FITTER
FASTER
STRONGER
SMARTER

FITTER FASTER STRONGER SMARTER

Miranda Banks

TRAINING FOR THE PERFORMANCE OF LIFE

Wrightbooks

BICENTENNIAL
1807
WILEY
2007
BICENTENNIAL

First published 2007 by Wrightbooks
an imprint of John Wiley & Sons Australia, Ltd
42 McDougall Street, Milton, Qld 4064

Office also in Melbourne

Typeset in Palantino LT 10.5/13.8pt

Banks, Miranda.

Fitter, faster, stronger, smarter: training for the performance of life.

Includes index.

ISBN-13: 9780731406630.
ISBN-10: 0 7314 0663 X.

1. Success. 2. Self-actualization (Psychology). I. Title.

158.1

Cover design: Brad Maxwell

Wiley Bicentennial Logo: Richard J Pacifico

Author photograph © John Wiley & Sons Australia/Taken by Kari-Ann Tapp

Cover image: Getty Images/Stock Illustration/Images.com

Phil Hogan's keys for success on pp. 207–208 © Phil Hogan

Printed in Australia by McPherson's Printing Group

10 9 8 7 6 5 4 3 2 1

Disclaimer
The material in this publication is of the nature of general comment only, and neither purports nor intends to be advice. Readers should not act on the basis of any matter in this publication without considering (and if appropriate taking) professional advice with due regard to their own particular circumstances. The author and publisher expressly disclaim all and any liability to any person, whether a purchaser of this publication or not, in respect of anything and of the consequences of anything done or omitted to be done by any such person in reliance, whether in whole or part, upon the whole or any part of the contents of this publication.

Contents

Contents *(cont'd)*

Foreword

It's not that some people have willpower and some don't. It's that some people are ready to change and others are not.

Dr James Gordon, MD

I first met Miranda Banks in Brisbane, Australia on a speaking tour. She attended a full-day conference during which I lectured about resilience and stress hardiness. From the moment she approached me with a question, I knew there was something special about Miranda. Perhaps it was the sparkle in her eye, the manner in which she posed her question or her engaging smile, but within a few moments of conversation I immediately knew she had some very interesting ideas about stress hardiness and reaching life goals. She shared some of her ideas with me, and I became intrigued by her fitter, faster, stronger, smarter (FFSS) model as a means of developing a resilient mindset and stress hardiness in life. So it is with great pleasure that I write this foreword to her first book.

Banks uses sports as a way to understand our mindsets. What can we learn from appreciating the history of sporting activities in our species? Is sport more than just entertainment for most and vocation for a few? An appreciation of the history of sports and humankind helps us understand the lessons learned through practice and skill development. These lessons can and do lend themselves well to everyday life.

Identifying mankind's first sporting activity is like trying to date the first time we walked upright, made a fire or used tools. Long before sport became a commodity, it was a useful way for people to develop and demonstrate mastery of their abilities over nature and the world around them. Sport involves a variety of basic human physical, cognitive and emotional skills. In the caves of France over 30 000 years ago, our ancestors provided evidence of sporting activities as they recorded their lives for posterity. These particular drawings do not show life sustaining activities such as hunting but rather portray ceremony and activity for the sheer sake of competition.

Sport has been one of few consistencies between myriad cultures spread throughout time and geography. When Captain Cook first visited the Hawaiian Islands in 1778 he reported the natives were 'surfing'. The ancient Mayan and Aztec civilizations played a variety of ball games, some with serious adverse consequences for the losers. The Native Americans engaged in games and sports as well. Long before the Europeans set foot in North America, American Indians were playing lacrosse-type ball games, running competitively and engaging in other activities of physical skill.

Individual sports, such as wrestling and archery, have been practiced across cultures and the world since ancient times. Artefacts and records suggest the Chinese engaged in sporting activities as long as 4000 years ago. For the Chinese, sporting activities were closely related to work, war and entertainment. Monuments to the Pharaohs suggest that there was a range of well-developed and well-regulated sports several thousands of years ago in Egypt, including swimming and Fishing. Along the Nile, sports included javelin throwing, high jump and wrestling. Many of these early activities bear a strong resemblance to non-sporting activities necessary for survival.

Of all of the ancient cultures, the Greeks are most closely associated with the development of sports. Wrestling, running, boxing, javelin, discus throwing and chariot racing were prevalent throughout their empire. The military culture of Greece appeared to exert a significant influence on the development of its sports. Sporting activities are described in Homer's *Iliad*. The Greeks developed the Olympic games, which were held every four years in ancient Greece, and the marathon. Winners of the games received honor throughout the empire and were often granted special status in the community. Increasingly, as sports became more organised, activities that were once necessary for survival became regulated activities completed solely for pleasure or competition.

Many modern sports can trace their roots back to the local games of the rural working class, while others find their origins in aristocracy. With the coming of the industrial revolution, and the movement of people from the country to the cities, rural games of sport moved to urban centres in which special fields were reserved for these activities.

The industrial revolution and mass production brought increased leisure time, which then allowed for spectator sports and greater accessibility for the masses. The advent of mass media and global communication allowed sports to become a professional, dedicated activity for some, and further drove the popularity of sporting activities. Every culture and time places its own stamp on sports, with our current culture developing technologically related sports, such as rock climbing or auto racing. In sum, sport truly imitates life.

Today athletic training has shifted to focus upon the mind as well as the body. It is increasingly recognised in professional sports that the difference between good and great may not lie merely in the coordination of muscles and eyes nor sheer physical strength, but in the mindset of the athlete. Suddenly sports have become as much psychological as physical activities. So it is not surprising that the sporting movement in mimicking life now borrows heavily from psychology and the self-help movement, which is any practice whereby an individual or a group attempts self-improvement.

Take, for example, the work of Norman Vincent Peale. Dr Peale wrote forty-six inspirational books, but *The Power of Positive Thinking*, first published in 1952 and by far his most widely read book, gave birth to the self-help movement. Peale's approach strongly reflected his belief that how we think affects what we do. Though Peale's detractors suggested that his single case examples, anecdotes and the stories from which he drew his ideas were hard to substantiate and that his claims that everyone could be successful was perhaps extreme, Peale's influence propelled the self-help movement. Today bookstores are replete with shelf after shelf of books offering sometimes science based but more often common sense suggestions on how to live a positive, stress hardy life. Though Peale founded his approach on a religious background, other self-help pioneers, such as Dr Albert Ellis, suggested that a person needed only rational, realistic and logical thinking to improve his or her life. Ellis' work spawned dozens of related models.

The homespun advice of Norman Vincent Peale has now developed into a worldwide, multibillion-dollar industry. Research and market data estimates the self-improvement market generated 8.5 billion dollars in sales in 2003, including infomercials, institutes, books, cassettes, DVDs, seminars, stress management and personal coaching. Estimates suggest that this industry will grow to over 11 billion dollars in sales by 2008. The concept of self-help has also found its way into wider circles in merchandising, self-checkout in the supermarket or pumping gas. But as with any concept, there are limits. These methods don't work for everyone. We continue to search for the true path to a happy, fulfilled life.

What really changes when we help ourselves? Is it our thoughts and feelings, or something physical like brain chemistry or even structure? Likely all four are changed. As Dr Richard Davidson of the University of Wisconsin in the United States points out, skills can be trained, and mastery leads to structural, enduring changes in the brain. Scientific evidence supports the Dalai Lama's belief, for example, that meditation changes the brain. Dr Michael Merzenich of the University of Southern California notes, 'We choose and sculpt how our ever-changing minds will work; we choose who we will be the next moment in a very real sense and these choices are left embossed on our physical selves'.

Just as psychology and the self-help movement have influenced sports, the lessons learned by participating in sports begin to influence life. *Fitter, Faster, Stronger, Smarter: Training for the Performance of Life* is a ground-breaking look at this phenomenon. The ten chapters in *Fitter, Faster, Stronger, Smarter* are built on a model of performance coaching; the model used by individuals and teams to facilitate improved performance. Performance coaching focuses on developing a plan of action aligned with individual or team goals. Then progress is monitored throughout the execution of the plan. Banks writes that the fitter, faster, stronger, smarter process is the structural component of performance coaching. It is the 'self' in self-help. Banks offers a road map to help readers appreciate and understand her model and put it to use in making personal change. Banks calls on traditional cognitive behavioral concepts to help readers examine their internal drives, motivation and the influences of their external environment in which they live, work and play. Athletes and non-athletes alike can benefit from applying Banks's model to their own lives.

Banks suggests that the FFSS mindset is based on the ability to reframe every problem, challenge or encounter in life by viewing these through an infinitely more manageable lens. She is not just interested in the outcome of adapting an athletic model to everyday life, she also appreciates that the destination is important only relative to the personal journey. She notes that this idea is the universal process that binds sporting champions, corporate successes and resilient people.

The guiding principle of Banks's work is that 'performance is a function of how well you achieve your goals'. As with any good guidebook, performance is tied not just to outcome but also to the process. Banks's model offers strategies to appreciate, understand and develop the qualities of resilient individuals. Success, as my colleague Dr Robert Brooks and I have noted repeatedly in our work, is equated with resilience but should not be confused nor considered solely dependant upon outcome or income. Success in life encompasses features including positive relationships with others, contentment at work and in our lives as a whole, and feelings of optimism.

The FFSS model is not just for those who want to dramatically change their lives, but serves as a framework for everyday life that gives us the tools to deal with the unexpected challenges and stress that we all encounter. Resilient individuals possess a set of assumptions or attitudes about themselves that influence their behaviours and development. In turn, these behaviours and skills influence this set of assumptions so that a dynamic process is constantly operating. We call this set of assumptions a mindset. A resilient mindset is composed of several main features, including:

- feeling in control of one's life

- knowing how to fortify one's stress hardiness

- being empathetic

- displaying effective communication and other interpersonal capabilities

- possessing solid problem-solving and decision-making skills

- establishing realistic goals and expectations
- learning from both success and failure
- being a compassionate and contributing member of society
- living a responsible life based on a thoughtful set of values
- feeling special but not self-centred, while helping others to feel the same.

Possessing a resilient mindset does not imply that one is free from stress, pressure and conflict but that one can successfully cope with problems as they arise. We also use the word mindset to capture an important premise. Mindsets can be changed. The FFSS framework offers one of the best sets of principles and strategies to guide the development of a resilient mindset. Though our unique life experiences influence our mindsets, they are not set in stone. The more we understand the beliefs and goals that guide our behaviours, the more successfully we can engage in the process of replacing counter-productive, self-defeating assumptions and behaviours with those that lead to a more resilient, fulfilling life.

As Banks writes, her book 'is designed to be a reference tool as well as a method to provoke your thinking'. She suggests that her book be considered 'a travel guide to your journey of performance through life'. As she rightly notes, 'Life is dynamic and the tools we use to assist us should reflect the same dynamism'. Banks eloquently points out that 'to master your future you first need to master yourself'.

Fitter, Faster, Stronger, Smarter is the gateway to this mastery and an effective means to train for the life you want to live.

Dr Sam Goldstein, PhD
Salt Lake City, Utah
May 2007

Acknowledgements

It was becoming apparent to me that to succeed, one must first master one's profession.

General Montgomery

My thanks go first to my own support team, without which this book would merely be a dream to be indulged in over a bottle of wine. To my friends—thank you for your support (Emma B and Tony J), for your advice (Angela S) and for allowing me to regularly tap into your professional expertise (Vicki W and Dean B). Thank you to my publisher, John Wiley & Sons, which took a chance on an unknown author and provided me with expertise, encouragement and a whole bucket load of patience. My enormous appreciation also goes to Bill Concannon, the highly successful and eminently marvellous managing director of bookstores all over Queensland, who educated me on the world of authors, books and readership—and who continues to generously tout my professional expertise at his golf club!

Thanks also to my family—to my 'mitey' mother for her inspiration and her approach to child raising (which fostered in her children an ability to believe in themselves); my brother, Donald and my sister, Lucy (and her partner, Chris); and to Godfrey, James and Amanda, and Susie, Steve and Summer (who make up the other half of our noisy clan in Australia). Thank you for providing the love, stability and bags of fun that fuelled me to be 'fitter, faster, stronger, smarter'.

To my mentor in the United States, Dr Sam Goldstein, your generosity of spirit is unflagging. Thank you for your brilliance as a psychologist, a fellow author and a person who revels in developing others.

Finally, to the champions in my book, you have kindly given your time, thoughts and stories to assist me with the material for *Fitter, Faster, Stronger, Smarter*. The people who contributed range from world-beating sportsmen (such as rugby players George Gregan and Elton Flatley) to internationally acclaimed sportswomen who've successfully made the transition from sport to business (like former Australian netball captain Vicki Wilson). I spoke with coaching and support staff whose longevity in the business and outstanding successes speak volumes. I also chatted with some exceptionally astute businesspeople from diverse backgrounds—including banking, leadership development and information technology. I've also included comments made by those who would be unaware of their contribution because their observations originated many years ago in the trenches of World War I and World War II.

I'm equally indebted to a number of individuals who would not claim any recognition for the outstanding expertise they offered. Their modesty camouflages the fact that they—like all people—have tips and approaches that can be used to make individuals more effective at the job they do or the people they want to be. I've interwoven those snippets of advice with the invaluable contributions from those broadly acknowledged as experts in their field.

I would like to suggest that all individuals have the capacity to be experts in their field, if they could simply decide on their goal and then plan their approach for getting there.

I'd like to thank, in alphabetical order, the following people:

- *Barb Barkley.* The current vibrant CEO of Womensport Queensland, Barb has also had the pleasure of working with renowned rugby league coach Wayne Bennett during her time with the Brisbane Broncos.

- *Dean Benton.* The highly respected performance coordinator for the Brisbane Broncos, Dean has worked as a trainer in elite professional and Olympic sports for many years. Dean is known for his high-performance outcomes as well as his commitment to continuing professional development and learning.

- *Barry Bull.* The proud owner of Toombul Music and an author in his own right, Barry now takes pleasure in assisting the successful development of others—both in and out of the retail sector.

- *David Croft.* A dedicated senior member of the Queensland Reds rugby team and a past Australian Wallaby, David now holds a number of business interests in addition to playing professional rugby.

- *Irene Darling.* My 'mitey' mother, who is a business owner, an accountant and a mother of three, is still capable of rolling over an outsize merino sheep and clearing a five-foot fence on a horse—and all before breakfast.

- *Ben Darwin.* A respected past Australian Wallaby prop, Ben sustained a serious spinal injury during an international game. He is now engaged in his other passion—coaching both rugby and business.

- *Roger Davis.* A past Australian Wallaby, Roger was also involved in the senior command of Citibank in Japan and the US for many years. Now he is Director of Rothschild and Chair of the Rugby Union Players' Association. He holds a keen interest in the development of rugby players after their rugby careers.

- *Archie Douglas.* An avid sporting fan and an irresistible raconteur, Archie and his brother Gordon founded and fed the PRD Realty success story. He continues to keep his toe in the water with Colliers PRD, but focuses now on developing those around him though mentoring.

- *Marty Duncan.* The delightfully distinctive owner of the successful Freestyle restaurants in Brisbane, Marty was a chef before deciding to make his dreams a reality—by combining fabulous desserts with flowers and art in his signature eateries.

- *Elton Flatley.* A former champion Australian Wallaby and a convivial yet highly effective fly-half for the Queensland Reds, Elton has fought his own battles with injury and has diversified his interests to include those outside the rugby field.

- *Cathy Freeman.* An Australian Olympic champion of the track, Cathy is also passionate about her love for her country and her people. She has spent considerable time working with charities and community groups since her retirement from competitive sport.

- *George Gregan.* Another Australian sporting champion, George has been the decisive captain of the Australian Wallabies for the last five years. He and his wife also own and run the aptly named By George cafes.

- *Kellie Hogan.* Kellie has been Sports Dietitian to Queensland Rugby, and she continues to provide her services to the Queensland Academy of Sport and the Australian Institute of Sport. These achievements are all the more notable considering she accomplished them all before the age of twenty-two.

□ *Phil Hogan.* Phil is the face of welcome and hospitality in some of the most popular and successful bars and restaurants in Brisbane city. He and his brother are the entrepreneurial Hogan Brothers—known for their inimitable skill at turning a business disaster into a business divine.

□ *Jenny Hyde.* Jenny is an equestrian athlete who represents England in the sport of showjumping. Showjumping is an expensive sport and, therefore, like many athletes, Jenny needs her full-time job to fund her sporting passion.

□ *Tony Johnston.* With an extensive history in television and radio, Tony is now the radio host for ABC on the Gold Coast. His warmth and genuine interest in people and places have made him a popular talkback host and celebrity guest at community events.

□ *Eddie Jones.* Eddie is the intensely committed and talented former head coach for the Australian Wallabies and the premier-winning ACT Brumbies. Displaying tenacity in the face of challenge from which many others would have run. He is now the head coach for the Queensland Reds,

□ *Bennett King.* Bennett is the personable, multiple Sheffield Shield–winning former Queensland Bulls cricket coach who now plies his trade as the national cricket coach for the West Indies.

□ *David Liddy.* David is the highly successful CEO of the Bank of Queensland. He is responsible for spearheading the bank's recent outstanding corporate achievements. David's policy of setting high standards and then empowering those around him has seen him bear the fruits of corporate success.

- *Stu Livingstone.* Stu Livingstone is the dedicated strength and conditioning trainer for the Queensland Reds. He held the same position for the ACT Brumbies rugby squad.

- *Dr Graeme Maw.* Dr Maw is the former high performance manager for British Triathlon. A sports scientist by profession, he previously headed up the performance program for the highly successful Queensland Academy of Sport swim squad. Graeme has established his credibility in British sport within a short time span—primarily due to his achievement of performance outcomes through hard work and an acutely perceptive, analytical approach.

- *Paul McLean.* A past Wallaby rugby legend, Paul is now the president of Australian Rugby Union. He has also been the president of Queensland Rugby and a director of Savills FPD. Paul's unassuming manner—but unassailable standards—have engendered success, respect and genuine affection in those around him.

- *Rob Metcalfe.* Rob is the magnetic and energetic CEO of Leading Initiatives Worldwide, a powerful performer in the competitive world of corporate leadership development. Rob was a member of the British Special Forces in a previous life and was commended in dispatches for his performance under fire.

- *Jeff Miller.* Jeff Miller is the former head coach for the Queensland Reds rugby team. He was also the assistant coach during the leadership of the Australian Wallabies by Rod Macqueen and a well-respected past Australian player in his own right.

- *Drew Mitchell.* Drew Mitchell is the much touted fullback for the Western Force Super 14 team and the Australian Wallabies. Still only a youngster, his natural talent has significantly benefited under the tutelage of Chris Latham.

- *Terry Oliver.* Terry is the current and popular Queensland Bulls cricket coach. After seeing the Bulls all the way to the last three finals in the Pura Cup, Terry helped Queensland to outright victory and brought the Cup back to Queensland in 2006.

◻ *John Reynolds.* John is on the board of directors for the Bank of Queensland and is the Chair of Queensland Cotton Holdings. John has been a strategic adviser to companies, universities and government bodies across Australia.

◻ *John Roe.* John is the current highly regarded captain for the Queensland Reds as well as an experienced Australian Wallaby player. John is also on the point of completing his studies in medicine.

◻ *Anthony Rushton.* This casually debonair international restaurateur finally returned to his native Brisbane to establish Butter Bistro—after setting up the glamorous eateries Blue and Ivory in Hong Kong.

◻ *Janine Shepherd.* Janine is the inspirational athlete who injured herself in a cross-training exercise—leaving her a paraplegic. She then went on to learn how to fly and how to instruct flying. Janine has been the subject of a film and is a motivational speaker and author in her own right.

◻ *Ben Tune.* Ben is a former Australian Wallaby, a current Queensland Reds rugby player and a business owner. His inimitable try-scoring style spawned a cult following of swallow-divers. Ben had undergone multiple knee reconstructions as well as other surgery, yet he remained focused on his target of returning to rugby at the elite level. He succeeded.

◻ *AnneMarie White.* AnneMarie is a respected sports journalist and media manager who has covered Olympic and Commonwealth games on multiple occasions. With a background in teaching, she used her tenacity and drive to carve out a career in a highly competitive field. AnneMarie's biggest challenge arrived when she was diagnosed with breast cancer. She fought it with the same vigour and is happily now in remission.

□ *Derek Williams.* Derek is the highly successful Executive Vice-President and Chair at Oracle Asia-Pacific/Japan. During his time at Oracle, he has significantly increased the company's market share through his personal performances, and has used his leadership skills to empower those in his team.

□ *Tony Wilson.* Tony is the much respected strength and conditioning coordinator for the Queensland Bulls cricket team and Australian Baseball. He has also worked with the Reds Rugby College in the same role. Tony combines his physical-training consultancy with his role as a director of a corporate team-development business.

□ *Vicki Wilson (OAM).* Vicki is the former captain of the Australian netball team. Awarded a Medal of the Order of Australia for her service to sport, she is a magnet for both sporting and corporate respect. Balancing her time between various board representations and her roles as the ambassador for Sport and Recreation Queensland and the head coach for the Queensland Firebirds netball team, Vicki's obvious talents as a player have seen her consolidate her expertise as a coach of people in and out of sport.

□ *Scott Wisemantel.* Scott is the skills coach for the Australian Wallabies and a coaching consultant for a number of teams. He has held that role for a number of years and has earned respect in a highly competitive environment. Scott's laid-back style belies his insistence on impeccable standards—enabling him to develop strong, effective relationships with players and staff alike.

Introduction

It's 30 000 BC and a misty predawn light is starting to trail its way into your cave. You're obviously the first awake because you can hear the rhythmic sound of heavy breathing coming from the other sleeping mats. As you yawn, stretch and contemplate the day to come, you notice that the fire has almost gone out at the mouth of the cave—not a positive sign of effective security.

Without warning, the silence is broken by a blood-curdling roar. A large lion pads into sight. It stops—its body filling the cave's entrance—and eyes you hungrily.

Right now, your survival—and the survival of the others still asleep—depends on whether you're thinking one of the following:

▫ 'I'm toast!'

- 'Great! I love pitting myself against giant carnivores! My super-charged, light-weight killer spear is handy, and I'm feeling strong.'

- 'Run! I'm trapped, darn it. Didn't I tell the builder that I needed that escape hatch fixed yesterday?'

- 'I wish I'd paid more attention in the "How to talk with lions" class.'

- 'I wonder if I should hide under the covers? If I can't see it, maybe it can't see me.'

- 'Where's Steve? He's always claiming to be the lion tamer. Now here is his chance.'

- 'Dear Moggins—hand-reared since a cub—is here for his breakfast. I just wish he'd turn down the volume on his wake-up call.'

In short, when people are faced with a challenge, they have behavioural choices from which to select. They can choose to give in to the challenge, fight it, run from it, reason with it, hide from it, pass it onto someone else or reframe it so that it no longer represents a challenge.

Although people may no longer be faced with quite the same life-or-death challenges, they still encounter metaphorical lions this side of the Ice Age. Their ability to manage them becomes crucial to their survival and success. That capability not only affects someone as an individual, but also the people around—and dependent on—that person. The approach people therefore take in the execution of their daily lives can carry considerable responsibility.

The fitter, faster, stronger, smarter mindset

The ability to plan for an encounter with a lion—or to reframe the encounter so that the lion becomes a kitten and is therefore infinitely more manageable—forms a significant component of the thinking that sets achievers and non-achievers apart. Sporting champions, corporate successes and resilient people understand this. They recognise a challenge and have strategies prepared to manage them; if those strategies aren't in place, they will turn the challenge to their advantage. And it's not just about encountering lions—it's also about getting to where they want to be in the most effective and efficient manner possible.

Successful people have a mindset that elevates them above the bodies wallowing in the pond of mediocrity. They:

- have better mental *fitness*—possessing a greater mental capacity to adapt to a given situation and a superior state of general mental wellbeing

- are mentally *faster*—being quicker at seeing a potential outcome and then obtaining it, at resolving challenges and at returning to their designated path

- are mentally *stronger*—having more power to resist attack or strain, and a greater capacity for effective action

- are mentally *smarter*—being characterised by a quick and perceptive thought process and a shrewd approach to dealing with people and situations

All in all, successful people have a 'fitter, faster, stronger, smarter' mindset than most.

So what if you were to gather together some of these people, ask them some questions about their strategies for achievement and put their answers in a framework that you could use for your individual benefit? It should, at the very least, make for some interesting reading.

What's in it for you

*I don't identify with people who don't want to learn; I have
nothing to say to them.*

Archie Douglas

The guiding principle of this book is that your performance is
a function of how well you achieve your goals. In other words,
your performance is your behavioural execution—it means using
your knowledge to achieve your goals, as distinguished from
merely possessing that knowledge. Regardless of the nature of
your goals—whether you want to be happier or healthier, or
achieve in business, sport or at home—fitter, faster, stronger,
smarter practices can impel you there with greater velocity. Elite
sportspeople set performance targets both on and off the sports
field, and then design and execute a program by which to achieve
them. That same attitude to performance is paralleled by the
successful elite in business and in life—demonstrating that people
can train as effectively for life as athletes train for Olympic glory.

As a performance coach working with professional sports teams,
elite amateur athletes and senior management personnel in
business, I've seen—time and time again—an overlap between
the principles for achieving success on the football field or netball
court and success in the boardroom or in life.

Principles and factors are all very good, but to make these pages
eminently more readable and relevant, I've included tales and tips
from those in the field. As a performance coach, I have had the
privilege of meeting and working with many people who have
achieved great success in varied arenas, but whose principles for
success are very similar. Offering you support, their stories and
opinions will provide you with real-life examples of people who
have implemented performance principles in their own lives.
Pointers for all those looking to improve their life performance
are contained in these pages.

Journeys need maps

Use this book to create and develop a 'success map'—a path to follow by which to achieve your goals. A success map is a one-page sheet that acts as a compass; it sets out your goals and how you're going to meet them. By following each stage on your path from start to finish, you'll set in motion an effective structure for getting to where you want to be.

Each of the following sections will help you construct your own success map—and you can choose to put it together in whatever way best suits you. The point to remember is it has to be tailored to you as an individual, and it has to act as a reminder and a guide. You should keep returning to it to review your progress and direction, just as you'd navigate with a compass on a long journey. Australian Bennett King, the head coach of the West Indian cricket team and the successful, former head coach of Queensland Cricket, refers to himself, in his coaching capacity, as 'the compass'. He clarifies by saying, 'I give the direction to the players; I'm the one who sets out how to get us there and I'm the one who resets direction when we start getting lost'. Many people don't have access to a coach to keep them on track in their life performance, but everyone can access their own success map.

A success map—if it's put together well and used effectively —acts like the directive component of coaching. Firstly, map your course towards achievement of your goals, and then regularly review your success map to keep you aligned to those goals and to re-align you when your path becomes cloudy. To give a clearer picture, there is an example of a success map framework in appendix A.

Much of what will appear in this book has probably been sitting in your brain all along, so most of it shouldn't come as a surprise. They are issues that you have likely pushed to the bottom of your importance pile and then forgotten—along with your New Year's fitness or life-balance resolution, or any other commitment you made long ago but let fall by the wayside. Reading through should trigger a resurfacing of your resolve to apply yourself to improving all important areas in your life. It will also enable you to discover some fresh perspectives and tools to integrate with your newfound resolve—helping you to stay on track.

For simplicity—and to reinforce a focus on performance development—this book is divided into chapters that include ponder points at the end of each one. They provide you with opportunities to focus your own reflections, and they include some suggested summarised directions for implementing the information you've absorbed in the relevant chapter. After contemplating those points, outline—in the form of a to do list—the things missing from your current portfolio of actions that you have identified as being significant to the achievement of your success.

At the conclusion of the book, compile and prioritise your to do list and it will provide you with much of the content for a detailed success map. It's then up to you to make the commitment to follow it.

Choose to change

He which hath no stomach to this fight, let him depart.

William Shakespeare, *Henry V*

Change, as a general rule, is not something that human beings do particularly well. They prefer the comfort of knowing the next line in the script and ensconcing themselves in beds of familiarity.

Change can upset your equilibrium because it usually means taking a step back from your daily existence and assessing if what you're doing is effective or not. Change is also hard work, so you need to prepare yourself for putting in more effort than usual during those periods of change. However, just as you can steel yourself to shift a heavy object, you can also ready your body and mind for the challenge of change.

Surfing or being dumped

Extensive research done with elite athletes, both professional and amateur, making the move from sport to another career path found that the transition was easiest for those who voluntarily made the move—they marked their wave, lined up the board and rode it to shore. By contrast, the research also showed that athletes who involuntarily departed from their sport often found themselves at a loss—dumped on the sandy bottom as the waves swept over the top of them. The impact of involuntary departure from sport can only be mitigated by athletes by planning for their next career step before the departure day actually arrives. The biggest challenge for athletes in this predicament is that life after sport is seen by them as less appealing than a life framed around their sporting pursuit. Life after sport is another world—another ball game with different rules and competencies. It's unfamiliar. It's usually the reason why some athletes can live in constant denial of retirement from their sport right up until the day arrives—thereby leaving them at the mercy of chance.

Corporate life isn't wildly different. Research has found that the average person will make about seven career changes—let alone job changes within each field—in a working life. Some of those changes may be straightforward; indeed, they may even be anticipated with pleasure. However, many are involuntary, unexpected, unattractive and unfamiliar. Therefore, considering that change is highly likely, you're in a far stronger position if you have prepared a plan or two, so you at least stand the chance of turning that change into an opportunity rather than an obstacle.

Do you create change or does it more frequently come up from behind and swamp you? The more control you have over change, the more comfortable you'll be with the processes. Most people have the power of choice—people are never too old to change.

It's true that time and practice embeds habits—particularly over long periods of time. But deeply embedded habits are comfortable—sometimes even perceived as safe—because the alternatives are unfamiliar and potentially challenging. In fact, you can subconsciously choose to forget that you even have a choice. However, once you are aware of the alternatives, you can learn to anticipate, manage and possibly initiate change to work it to your advantage.

As mentioned earlier, change is a state that is inherently effort intensive, even if that change is positive. Knowing that you're likely to feel stress, even when you're experiencing positive change, can provide welcome relief from confusion you may feel. People often assume that they shouldn't be stressed when they're experiencing change for the good. But any change is stressful—and once you know this, it will encourage you to deal with your stress, rather than denying it because you think it's foolish to feel it.

For example, you may have just achieved that much coveted promotion at work or been awarded the best and fairest award at the end of your sporting season, and as a result you become a role model to those aspiring to do the same. Your mind would have to adapt to the increased pressure placed on you, role-related change and even a change in your environment. Those issues inflict stress on the body's systems—even when the changes bringing them about are positive overall.

It also makes sense that when change is negative, the pressure is increased because you usually have to manage the energy-draining impact of the change on your emotional, social and, often, financial resources. Whether positive or negative, change places stress on you.

Change is often something that people will try to avoid right up until their backs are against the wall. In trying to avoid it—like some athletes post-retirement—their ability to adapt post-change will be doubly difficult. So if they haven't planned or prepared for it, ultimately they won't adapt well. Many people lose valuable time by trying to put themselves back on track instead of just being able to 'hit the ground running'. That is, if you've done your preparation in advance and worked out the steps to take beforehand, you'll minimise the time you spend on the 'changeover' and feel far more confident about your new direction.

It's not just about saving time on your journey of life either. When presented with no option but to change and do it immediately, you can feel backed into a corner. People have a different mindset when they feel their backs are against the wall. When animals are cornered, even the most even-tempered creatures can turn into snarling balls of teeth if they feel under threat—even to hands that wish to help. Have you ever found yourself in the position in which—despite being aware that the person reaching out to you is trying to help—you feel so pressured that you just want to lash out? And when you have lashed out, did you promptly feel unbelievably guilty? By confronting situations requiring review and change, you're minimising the chance of finding yourself feeling trapped and under attack.

Finally, you need to know the reason for your change. Are you changing because you want to change or because you think you should? I'll talk more about this later in the chapter, but it's still important at this stage for you to ask yourself, 'Why am I doing this? Why do I want the target at the end?' Unless that answer has sufficient power and drive to carry you through the moments of self-doubt, frustration and challenge, then your decision to change is set on foundations of sand rather than rock—and when you encounter challenges, that sand will wash out. Common obstacles to change cited by people include a lack of time and resources, no inclination or support from others, and no immediacy of results. There is also the challenge of fatigue—sometimes making changes to the norm seems like too much hard work. Consciously consider each one of those hurdles in terms of your own situation and work out a practical approach to defeating each one. If you haven't factored them in, then your best intentions are likely to be walloped by the first challenge that rears its head. If you want a propitious start to the journey along your success map, make sure you conduct thorough groundwork.

Performance coaching

Performance coaching is about working with people to facilitate their goal achievement. The emphasis is on taking a collaborative approach—performance coaches are the experts on strategies and frameworks and the people being coached are the experts on their own characteristics, drives and ambitions. By working with those being coached in a dynamic environment of mutual trust, coaches can help their students to develop the planning, behaviours and mindsets—in other words, a success map—required to achieve their targets. Performance coaches—acting as a support and a monitor of progress—would then continue that coaching partnership through the execution of the map.

Why performance coaching is useful

Performance coaching is handy for a number of reasons. First, the coach would have you focus on what your goals are and in what priority they exist. Once you know the direction you're heading in, you can focus your energy on working towards your targets without distraction.

You only have a limited amount of energy—and unless you focus, it will, like water in a colander, head off in too many directions.

Second, a coach would work with you to develop and frame your individualised success map. You would then know where you're going and how to get there—and because it's designed with you and your abilities in mind you're more likely to believe you're capable of executing it.

Third, a coach would help you develop your own tool kit of strategies to speed up the pace at which you achieve your targets. These tools would also assist you to anticipate and manage challenging situations when they arise.

Fourth, a coach would be able to monitor your progress. In the same way that football players are not left to their own devices in the gym, a coach encourages best performance and staying on task by initiating regular review sessions. In fact, all the research that's been done on behavioural adherence has indicated that a plan is most stringently followed just prior to and just after a visit by the person monitoring progress.

Finally, a good coach—in conjunction with acting as a monitor—would also be a reminder to do the essential maintenance activities, such as nudging you to take time to 'sharpen the axe', so to speak. Just as you wouldn't expect to split a ton of firewood efficiently with the same blade without regular maintenance, you also wouldn't expect to perform at your best without continuous upkeep. That may include things like effective recovery activities, a resetting of goals or a change in focus.

When people become caught up in the frantic rhythm of daily life, they often forget to take time to maintain themselves or their success map—to 'sharpen the axe'. Coaching can provide a 'heads-up'—a recommendation that you stop for a moment and ensure you're on track and feeling capably sharp.

So where does the fitter, faster, stronger, smarter (FFSS) approach fit into this book and the performance coaching picture? Simply, FFSS is a program of training without the physical presence of a coach. If you work with me—through this book—on improving your performance, you will use the FFSS approach to speed up the achievement of your target performances. If you want to achieve your goals more effectively, FFSS is the process by which to do it; this book talks you through it, just as if I were coaching you.

The fitter, faster, stronger, smarter system

There are more models of behaviour than there are feathers on a pheasant, but a useful model must provide a framework through which to explain phenomena. Two rules for good models exist—accuracy and parsimony. In other words, an effective model needs to be spot on and simple. I chose to develop my own model based on research in the field, my learning and also my experiences as a performance coach. It's proved a useful tool on which to base performance development for individuals and teams.

There are two main parts to the system—'What? Where? How?' and 'T3'. The first half of the system is covered in part I of this book, and the second half of the system is covered in part II. Part III provides you with real-life stories from high-performing people who have overcome adversity in life to find success.

In each section I'll pose some questions and offer strategies that can be implemented for different reasons and at different occasions. That way, you'll develop your own kitbag into which you can delve when the need arises.

What? Where? How?

In part I, you start by asking yourself three simple questions:

1 What am I aiming for?

2 Where am I at now?

3 How am I going to get there?

Look at your goals first—the motivating forces behind the reasons for your effort—because you should find them most exciting. Goals give your efforts direction and a reason for being. Once you know where you're heading, you'll be able to accurately evaluate whether your other internal drivers of behaviour are aligned with that direction or whether you need to tinker around with them to obtain that alignment. Having a goal-achievement orientation is vital. Athletes are devoted to the setting of goals for the obvious reason that it works. In fact, research with Olympic athletes found that the difference between athletes who won gold medals and those who didn't was that the medal winners set goals for training sessions as well as for competition. The lesson here is you should set little everyday goals as well as big ones if you want to win gold.

You need to look at your current circumstances because they provide you with a starting point from which to move. If you're unaware of the exact nature of your current circumstances and needs then you may overlook some essential factors in planning your pathway and therefore hit obstacles quickly.

The 'how' of getting to your goals is the complex stage, so you need to take time to explore your options and evaluate them before deciding on a definitive plan. To manage the complexity of comprehensively answering how you can achieve our goals, move on to part II and use the T3 process.

Targets one, two and three (T3)

The abbreviation T3 stands for target one, target two and target three. The references to 'target' give you a focus point for your attention.

Target one encompasses *your internal drivers of behaviour.* In part II, you'll take a closer look at how you're going to get to where you want to be. You'll examine what drives your behaviour from the inside—what it is you believe in, and what you're feeling, thinking and capable of doing. How are those factors currently influencing your behaviour and how might you alter the workings of those factors so you can be better aligned with your goals?

What pushes you from the inside to behave in a certain way? What you think and how you feel at any given time are significant drivers of your behaviour. Whether you believe you possess the knowledge and ability to execute a particular behaviour will also impact outcomes. Underlying all of these are your values — which remain fairly stable over time. As an example, imagine you are making a presentation to a potential group of sponsors and that you have two options by which to react:

1   You know your goal is to secure support from sponsors for the organisation by making the right pitch in your presentation. At the moment, you have all the material ready to go. What's happening on your inside? You may be thinking, 'This is a huge job. I can't believe they gave it to me — it must have only been because my manager is away. Last time I did one of these, I severely stuffed up. It could happen again and completely devastate everything!' If those are your thoughts, then it's pretty likely that your feelings are horribly negative — you're feeling anxious and worried that things won't go well or that you'll be embarrassed, or you simply don't want to be doing it. You may have some basic presentation skills, but you perceive that those skills are likely to let you down. All in all, it's a recipe for self-fulfilling doom.

2   You may actually be thinking, 'Wow! What a challenge! I know it's a huge responsibility, but I back myself to do it well. My manager must have real faith in me since he's scheduled it during his absence. I'm going to show him that his faith is well-placed'. In this case, your feelings are likely to be those of excitement and perhaps some apprehension laced with a positive, 'can do' attitude. You recognise that your basic presentation skills will be tested, but you believe that they'll be good enough to do the job — and you throw in some enthusiasm for good measure. This result, on the other hand, is a recipe for self-fulfilling success.

Unsurprisingly, the FFSS approach aims to cultivate the second version of events because version one isn't aligned to achieving the goal of securing sponsorship, but version two is.

Moving on from the elements of target one, target two focuses your attention on the *external drivers of your behaviour*—who and what in your life affects how you behave. People don't live in a vacuum, but, rather, they interact with people, places and things around them. To maximise the chances of a positive result emerging from those external factors, you need to understand the nature, direction and size of their influence. So do they assist you along your path to goal achievement or do they hinder your progress? Can you mitigate their impact or do you need to learn how to better manage them?

Who are the people, places and things that influence you for good or for bad? Do you surround yourself with people who energise you or who suck you dry? Is there a chance for you to maximise your time with energisers and minimise your time with energy drainers? As with the rest of nature, there are peak environments in which you most easily achieve your best results. For example, generally it's easier to grow mangoes in Queensland's heat and sunshine and grow apples in Tasmania's cool and temperate climate, but both fruits can probably be grown in either state if the environment is made conducive to their growth. Nothing is beyond the realms of possibility if the environment is correct—visitors to the Gold Coast's SeaWorld, for example, have the opportunity of watching polar bears at play despite the tropical heat. Why? It's simply because SeaWorld polar bears are provided with an environment in which they can thrive.

People flourish best in their natural habitat—are you an 'indoors' person or 'outdoors' person? Do you work best as leader or follower? Where do you speak your mind? When do you prefer to stay quiet? For periods of time, however, people need to perform effectively outside of that natural habitat. For example, you might have just moved interstate for work reasons or joined a team that doesn't feel as comfortable as the last. Consequently, you'll need to put in place some things in order for you to perform effectively out of your peak operating environment. They can range from communication processes to your 'escape hatch' for times of turbulence. To make those changes, you need to be aware of, understand and have the capacity to alter the people, places and things that affect you. If change isn't possible, then you need some effective recharge strategies to bring your energy levels back up again.

Finally, there is target three—*behaviour alignment*. Which behaviours are aligned to your goal pathway? Are those behaviours positively feeding back into your internal drivers to compound your successful progress? If not, what can you do to put yourself back on track? You need to identify the behaviours that aid the achievement of your goals and compare them with your current behaviours. What effect do different behaviours have on you? As funny as it sounds, your current behaviour can affect the likelihood of certain future behaviours.

Discussing that concept further, using one form of behaviour can result in another—such as 'talking yourself into' doing something. The principle of behaviour begetting behaviour is one of the reasons why the use of key words or phrases is so useful in sporting competition—for example, several athletes with whom I work employ the phrase 'feel the flow' to drop their anxiety levels and slide into a relaxed yet highly productive state.

To illustrate another way in which behaviour can instigate other related behaviours, consider the references some people make to 'being on a roll' or 'riding the wave of momentum', implying that one behaviour leads to another, to another, to another and so on. Behaviours build on their outcomes, so when you do something and feel good about its outcome, you will keep heading in that same direction. The problem is it can work for you or against you—for good or for evil. Take the example of a woman who rises in the morning to go for a stout walk. The act of walking propels her into her day; she feels more energised, confident and relaxed—so she ends up being far more productive. However, that same woman also decides, on occasion, that it's too dark, cold or unappealing to walk that morning. As a consequence, on those days she complains of feeling sluggish, and of having lower energy levels and a reduced capability. She is therefore less likely to feel as productive. Do your behaviours propel you into your day with vim and vigour or do they leave you wishing for more caffeine in your daily cuppa?

Close analysis of targets one, two and three will tell you how you should accomplish your goals. Aligning your goals to the forces within you and around you will enable you to create and refine your success map.

Understanding the elements of the FFSS performance coaching model enables you to take a structured and focused approach to performance development.

Ponder points

➽ Be aware that—whether change is good or bad—it will drain your energy levels, so make sure your energy is increased for that period.

➽ The more control you feel you have over the processes of change, the easier the transition will be for you.

➽ Be clear about why you're making the change— you need motivation that is strong enough to support you as you navigate the storms and pitfalls that you'll encounter along your journey.

➽ You have the power to make change happen— if you choose to do so.

Ponder points (cont'd)

➤ One of the biggest keys to success is having a plan that is well considered, practical and realistic, and relevant to you and your situation at this point in time.

➤ The role of performance coaching is to facilitate goal achievement through a team approach between coach and client.

➤ Performance coaching maximises goal achievement in a number of ways.

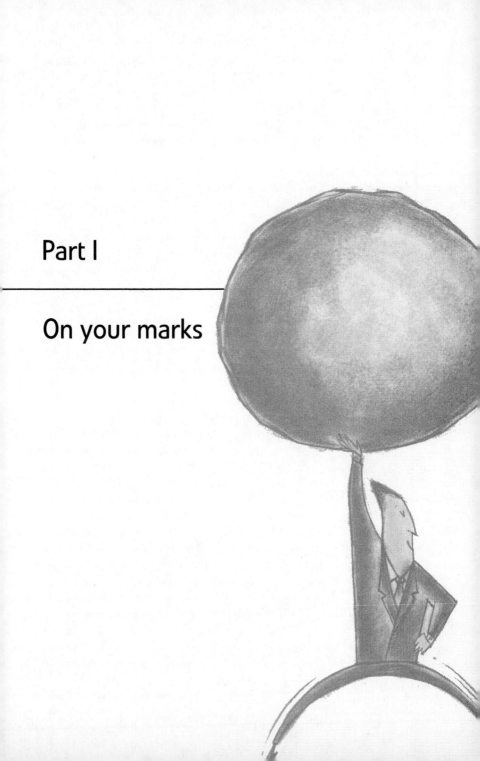

Part I

On your marks

Chapter 1

What are you aiming for?

Knowing the reason for your intentions enables you to set your goals within the context of that purpose. Rob Metcalfe, Chief Executive Officer (CEO) of Leading Initiatives Worldwide, a global leadership-development organisation, knows about the necessity of fully understanding one's purpose. He says:

> With purpose, your goals are inextricably linked. Purpose is something that is never achieved, but our goals towards that purpose are very much achievable. For example, the purpose of our organisation is to leave a legacy of leadership.

> We then set goals related to achieving that purpose within a given organisation. When we achieve those goals, we reset our next goals in alignment with our continuing purpose of leaving that legacy of leadership.

Barb Barkley, the youthful CEO of Womensport Queensland, echoes Rob's sentiments:

> Your purpose must be in your heart. That way it can act as a guide for all your choices: if you divert a ship by a mere two degrees, you'll end up in a completely different part of the world.

The same philosophy can be applied to you as an individual. How would you answer the question, 'What is my purpose?' How strongly does it sit in your heart? Does it actively perform as a guide for your choices?

Knowing your purpose also helps you to construct your goals as accurately and realistically as possible. 'Sport is interhuman competition. It's not about racing the clock; it's about who is first over the line', says Dr Graeme Maw, the former high performance manager for British Triathlon. He elaborates:

> Paul Tergat is the marathon world champion. The guy who came in second place broke the existing world record, but he didn't win the race so got nothing. You have to clearly understand your outcome: if you want to be the best in the world, then winning the race is more important than breaking the world record.

Terry Oliver, Head Coach of the Queensland Bulls cricket team, says, 'Setting goals is necessary since you use your goals as a beacon to know your direction. I never thought that I'd be coaching Queensland. I just knew that I loved coaching and the game'. Terry has a purpose or—as he refers to it—a philosophy of 'aiming to help people to help themselves'. He reveals:

> I just stuck to my philosophy and made goals within my control. There are lots of things that are outside people's control in sport and business—how you choose to deal with each punch and each opportunity is vital. With every punch, you have to get up, dust yourself off and move forward one more time—and head towards that beacon again.

BOMOAGs, visions and dreams

If a man does not know to which harbour he is heading, then no wind is the right wind.

Lucius Annaeus Seneca

Most people have a vague picture in their mind of what they're aiming for. Some of them are better at creating that picture than others—a fact brought home to me when I was up in northern Queensland visiting one of the regional rugby colleges. Kellie Hogan, the dietitian for Queensland Rugby, and I used to do a roadshow there once a year to speak to the players within our programs.

It was a scorcher of an afternoon in Rockhampton that day; the air-conditioning unit was doing its best to provide some respite from the heat in Rockhampton Rugby Club, where our regional college players—most of them still in their school uniforms—were gathered.

I told them to close their eyes and then I asked each of them, 'What's your rugby dream? Where are you? What do you see yourself doing?' Most of the boys had a rough picture in their mind, but a couple of them really lived it. One lad, in particular, said:

> I'm running out of the tunnel onto Ballymore. I'm wearing a Reds jersey and we're about to play New South Wales. I've got butterflies in my stomach and my boots are a bit on the tight side, but I can hear the crowd going off and I'm feeling awesome. It's my first game for Queensland and the crowd are cheering for me!

The value that he placed on his rugby dream wasn't just evident from the detail he gave me, but also from the passion in his voice when he said it. At that point in time, no-one in the room held any doubt that he would one day do it. Every time I tell that story, I get goose bumps.

Most people know what it means to have a dream, though they may not want to acknowledge its existence. However, the very nature of the word 'dream' suggests a set of circumstances that is otherworldly and removed from the reality of living. For coaching purposes, you need to remove those connotations so that you can begin to see your dream as a goal — a huge one that is often grounded in the long term. That dream, your main goal, is your BOMOAG.

Your BOMOAG is your big overriding mother of a goal. It's the carrot at the end of your current path, the desired outcome pictured in your head and the vision that keeps you inspired even when the going gets tough. For the vision to be effective, you have to live it. You have to feel what it's like to achieve that dream — and practise 'living' it in your mind daily, just like that schoolboy from Rockhampton Rugby Club.

Knowing your goal

Many people cannot spring out of bed and announce to themselves and the world that they know their BOMOAG — and it's not because they're not vocalising types, but because they simply don't know what it is. When I ask clients about their vision, the response I frequently hear is, 'What's my vision? I honestly have no idea!' Interestingly, on further investigation, I usually discover that there is indeed a vision, but not perhaps the one that the person feels it should be. Sometimes people feel the pressure to achieve in an area they don't really believe in or enjoy because of the expectations of others. Often it's because it was once their vision, but as circumstances have changed, their original vision hasn't.

Alternatively, people may not have a definitive BOMOAG, but instead possess a loose concept — a rough idea of wanting to be a certain way, such as wanting to 'be happy'. When this happens with my clients, I then pose the question, Well, what does that feel like and look like? When do you feel happy? What are you doing?

Who are you with? Where are you? What are you thinking?' We can then start to build a picture of what it means to be a certain way for them—that's the key. I can't assume to know what would make others happy—they need to tell me how it is for them.

Sometimes it's easier to start with a short-term vision if you're struggling to nail that BOMOAG for yourself. Break the big picture of life into bite-sized chunks. In other words, address how you'd like to be, to feel and to act in each part of your life. Then start to build each individual goal picture. Who's around you? Where are you? What are you doing? What are you thinking? Make each picture in your head as clear as possible. Sometimes when I work with people, I encourage them to draw the different elements that come to mind with each mental picture, or I ask them to use a collage of images taken from printed material. The most important aspect of the process to remember is that each goal along the pathway should match your overall vision, your BOMOAG—something real and relevant, and about which you feel strongly.

When I coach senior management, I often ask the question, 'How would you like to be described by others?', and I then use that response as a platform from which to develop a leadership BOMOAG. The clients can then start to build a clear picture of the types of leaders they aspire to be. Always take the time to build your goal pictures clearly because they become the foundation stones on which to base your behaviours.

The clarity of the picture in your mind is vital—especially if the path to getting there is going to take longer than a couple of days. A common example of how this operates is of a person who comes to see me because he wants to lose weight. I'll call him Eric. The first thing I ask is 'Why?' Eric replies with answers that range from health reasons to improving his golf game. He adds that only eighteen months ago he was much fitter and weighed fifteen kilograms less. I ask Eric to close his eyes and describe how he sees himself when he's met his goals. He tells me that he sees himself on the golf course, wearing clothes that are comfortable, and feeling and looking fit. In particular, he tells me he can see himself feeling much more energised when he takes his shots, rather than his carting around a lot of useless weight for no reason. Eric's picture is a good one because it's clear and he's passionate about it. I tell Eric I want him to practise 'seeing' that picture of himself daily—especially when he's faced with food or exercise choices that require him being prodded in the right direction. Happily for Eric, he gets it and maintains his healthy lifestyle program with enthusiasm, despite his time-consuming role as head of a leading franchise organisation.

For those who are struggling to decide whether to take one direction over another—such as choosing a rugby career over a cricket one, university over a trade apprenticeship, accepting a promotion over changing companies or leaving a relationship instead of staying and trying again—my suggestion is to first gather as much information as you can about the end state of each option. How would your day most likely unroll? What lifestyle changes would each option entail? What challenges or sacrifices would you be faced with?

Gather as much information as you can and use it to create a picture in your mind that is as clear as possible. Be aware of your response to each picture and then, finally, make your decision. Sometimes it can help to have input from others, but not to the extent that you leave the decision making to them. Only you can really know how you feel about the picture in your head. Derive confidence from the fact that you've put the effort into research and remember that you can only make decisions based on information available to you at the time—after all, vision is only 20/20 in hindsight.

What you are really giving away

Remember too that there's no such thing as not making a decision. By not acting, you're still making a decision not to strive in a particular direction—and in so doing, you are choosing to run with the status quo. The trap is that by withdrawing your energy from determinedly moving in any direction, others can wrest control from you—leaving you as the weed, rather than the surfer, on the wave.

Take the example of a Queensland Reds player I met a couple of years ago. He'd had a fairly ordinary playing season due to serious injury and was up for recontracting. Being a young chap—and perhaps feeling a lack of confidence in contractual negotiations—he gave all his negotiating power to his player agent. The player wasn't even present in the room during negotiations. When he was presented with the option of remaining with the Reds or being contracted to another state, his agent took control and almost lost the contract option of greater preference to him due to misunderstandings. Fortunately, the player eventually realised what was happening and re-assumed sufficient control over the situation to avert disaster. However, it might not have ended so well—demonstrating that there are many lessons to be learned by those who give control of their life or career to others.

Avoiding the effort of decision making by handing over control of it to others, can sometimes be very tempting, but control can be a powerful tool and, once given away, it can be mighty hard to regain. Think long and hard before you do so. Also, for areas unfamiliar to you in which you recruit experts specifically for their informed decision making—such as in medical, financial, vocational and spiritual spheres—ensure that you understand all the elements of the process along the way and the potential outcomes of doing so.

Leaving the decision making to someone else may seem the easy option, but history should tell you that people, for reasons fair or foul, may not always lead you in your preferred direction. In other words, always keep a firm hand on your own steering wheel, so to speak, even though you may occasionally choose to take some navigational advice from others.

Pressure makes diamonds

When you set goals for yourself, it's equally important to set timelines within which to achieve those goals. It creates a terminus that you can focus on; it also allows you to evaluate whether those goals are realistic. If you're sufficiently detailed in your plan and projected execution, then it's easy to run through your anticipated progress and evaluate whether you've allowed sufficient time to achieve your desired outcome.

For example, Ben Darwin, past prop for the Australian Wallabies with twenty-six test-matches to his name, tells another story of a schoolboy with a dream:

> I had two overriding goals: one was to play Australian Schoolboys and the other was to play for the Wallabies. I had a gold jersey made up with a line down the middle. On one side was written my name with the Australian Schoolboys logo; on the other was my name with the Australian Wallabies logo. I set myself those goals, gave myself sufficient time to do what I needed to do to achieve them and told everyone what I was aiming for. I achieved both of those goals within the time that I'd set.

Similarly, Jeff Miller, the former head coach of Queensland Rugby, outlines the importance of having a very strong vision of where you're heading and the time allocated to do it in: 'Once you have a strong vision for where you're going, you can then set goals to achieve that vision'.

He recalls working as an assistant Wallaby coach with Rod Macqueen leading up to the 1999 Rugby World Cup: 'Rod painted a vision for how he wanted us to play. We then set goals over a two-year period that allowed us to get there'.

Training and competition schedules are derived according to a four-year Olympiad. Most Olympic sports teams, squads and individuals work on a four-year plan that is based on that. Achievement at the Olympic Games is the usual BOMOAG for most eligible athletes. However, four years can seem like an eternity, so athletes often divide the time into sections that include smaller goals to maximise their motivation and intensity.

Timelines that can be divided into sections enable you to evaluate how realistic your goals are and provide you with greater opportunity to improve your drive and direction —because you're meeting milestones along the way.

Kept in sight—kept in mind

Once your BOMOAG has been set and your time parameters clarified, it's essential to provide constant reminders of your BOMOAG. When a rocket is heading to the moon, only 5 per cent of that time is spent accurately on the path to the moon; the other 95 per cent is spent on re-adjusting and re-aligning to that path. People are somewhat similar. They have plenty in their lives that serves to nudge them away from their original path, so they need regular reminders to re-align themselves to their target.

It's no different in business. David Liddy, CEO of the Bank of Queensland, talks about taking the reins at the bank seven years ago:

> We needed to re-think where it was we were heading. We needed to be clear on our purpose and our goals. We spent considerable time clarifying those—what exactly were they? What would they look like when we achieved them? Once we'd done that, I ensured that on every piece of correspondence that went out to staff, there'd be some reference to our main target goal and at every meeting, we'd talk about it.

David is highly respected within the business community because in five years he transformed the Bank of Queensland from an organisation facing stagnation into Australia's fastest growing retail bank. One of his key changes stemmed from his initial clarification of his BOMOAG and his constant referral to it.

As demonstrated by David's story, by constantly referring to your BOMOAG—by seeing it, hearing it and talking about it—you will possess the capability to regularly check whether your behaviours are directed towards achieving it. David Liddy further demonstrates how this applied at the Bank of Queensland:

> I made sure that everyone knew our main goal, that they all knew how they contributed to that goal and that they all had key performance indicators linked to that goal. I'd rather over communicate if it means we remain focused.

> We never want to run second, so we measure ourselves against other banks on a weekly basis—which is reinforced through weekly executive meetings—and make corrections to our path when required

Equally, having your BOMOAG uppermost in your mind can act as a powerful motivator during times of stress and challenge. When times are tough—when you're tired and cranky or frustrated with others around you—pull out your BOMOAG. If you've taken time in its selection, that vision will remind you why you're making all that effort.

Ownership of your BOMOAG

If your success is not on your own terms, if it looks good to the world, but doesn't feel good in your heart, it is not success at all.

Anna Quindlen

Your BOMOAG needs to inspire you—not your boss, your mother or society. You need to own your BOMOAG as passionately as the young schoolboy from the Regional Rugby College in Rockhampton did.

George Gregan, the captain of the Australian Wallabies, believes it is essential that everyone in a team—whether a national side or a state side—takes ownership of his or her goals. According to

George, that process is best achieved by involving the entire team in goal development. He states:

> We get everyone involved with goal setting because ownership is vital. Ownership means we start believing in the goal, so everything we do is moving towards achieving it—and it starts from the moment that goal is set.

Ownership of your BOMOAG also helps when you have to do things that you dislike in order to achieve your desired outcome. For example, Wallaby fly-half Elton Flatley—who also holds one of the best kicking records for Super 12 rugby—didn't really enjoy goal-kicking practice when he started out, saying:

> John Connolly (then the Queensland Rugby head coach) said that if I wanted to be the top number ten, I had to increase my goal-kicking accuracy. My goal was very much to be the top number ten. I was lucky to meet Ben Perkins who worked with John Eales on his kicking and he made training fun and enjoyable. I learned to kick accurately, I learned to enjoy it and my confidence grew.

Elton's team mate, veteran Wallaby winger Ben Tune, echoes those sentiments by saying, 'Training is just a means to an end. I don't enjoy training, but I enjoy what training can do for me'. In other words, Ben is always fully aware of his personal reasons for training—thereby giving him the motivational wherewithal to get in there and do it.

As Executive Vice-President and Chairman at Oracle Asia-Pacific/Japan, Derek Williams understands how essential goal ownership is. Here he explains how he encourages it:

> We're a young industry that's full of young people. We also need a blend of creativity and process. I try to promote a 'this is my company' feeling through talent recognition, giving a sense of accountability and self-responsibility. We run leaders' forums where the top talent within the firm come together. We give them the overall target state and ask them to sit down and

work out how to achieve it—then utilise those ideas in the planning cycle.

I also like to give pretty immediate recognition to excellence; a person can walk into one of those forums with one role and walk out having been promoted to another.

Oracle, a successful multinational organisation, obviously identifies the impact that goal ownership can have on individual and collective output so encourages it through reward. You need to recognise the influence that ownership over your personal BOMOAG can have on your output. That output then becomes its own reward.

Some people—particularly those starting out on their career path—can be swayed by the popular ideas and expectations endorsed by society. 'You've got to be careful about what heroes you choose,' advises Phil Hogan, a successful Brisbane businessperson who frequently uses Warren Buffett as a role model in his business practices. Providing a snapshot of his own experience in the business world, Phil continues:

> When I was in my mid twenties, I was the youngest director of a public company in Australian history. Back then, my heroes were people like Christopher Skase. Things have changed a lot since then. Now my heroes are people like Pat Rafter—he's one of Australia's great athletes, but he's also a great bloke who has his feet on the ground. I believe in surrounding myself with good people and Pat is now a stakeholder in our Jade Buddha business.
>
> I used to work alongside an extremely successful businessman. He was really successful in business, but it seemed to me that his life was less fulfilling. Society often tells us that we're successful if we make a lot of money and we can even be formally acknowledged for it. I just wonder, what's the point of having money if your family life is no good? That just doesn't work for me. I set my goals with a clear view in my mind of my 'holistic success'—of who it is that I personally want to be.

Phil is a smart guy. He shapes his goals and priorities on the issues that are important to him. Family happiness and holistic success are seen as non-negotiable by him; he sets his goals based on his sense of what is important. Although his work plays a pivotal role in his life, it does not take priority over time spent with his family.

For others, family concerns are less of a priority. In other words, it's not a matter of you sitting in judgement about what should and shouldn't be important. It's about seriously thinking about each area of your life and prioritising each one based on what's important to you. Many people fall down when they haven't stopped to take the time to do this for themselves. Drew Mitchell, one of the youngest players in the Australian Wallabies squad, summarises this beautifully:

> If there was advice that I'd give to the players trying to break into the side, I'd tell them to be true to yourself. Don't do something just because you think others want it. Trust your instinct and do what you think is right rather than mould yourself around what you think people like. Don't play it safe — unless playing it safe really is you.

Take all advice with a handshake and a pinch of salt

Fortune favours the brave.

Virgil

Whether personal or professional, changes in life direction can all too often be open to the overt influence of others. There are a vast number of people who are sufficiently content sitting in mediocrity and lack the inclination to rise above it. Those same people can at times resent the will and fire of others to leave mediocrity behind. Others can discourage you from a particular path because of their own underlying belief that the path is too hard — if it is too hard for them, then they assume it would be too hard for you.

My good friend and successful media personality Tony Johnston had some great words when I was pondering my own future path:

> Nothing should impede any options or possibilities. You will find that others always impose their fears on your thoughts or plans. Stick to your truth and what feels right.

You should assess all advice—whether it is asked for or not—within the context of your own goals, skills and timing. Sometimes it's a matter of listening to your gut instinct, but that can be coloured by low self-belief. So if you have a worry or a fear about a certain pathway, perhaps it's because it's the wrong one. Then again, perhaps it's because your inner voice is drowning out your self-confidence in a wave of self-bashing. How can you really tell which way is the best?

Having a clear pathway that includes realistic progress goals along the way, will enable you to reasonably assess whether your chosen path is indeed too hard. Once the path is assessed as realistic and desired, you're then faced with two options—you can either listen to the doomsayers and abandon the plan or use their words as a challenge to fire yourself up. However well intended any advice, being able to objectively assess its validity and weigh it up against your knowledge and feelings is a vital skill. Take even the most well-meaning advice with a handshake of appreciation, but also with a hefty pinch of salt.

There is an infinite list of examples of 'well-meaning advice'. Among the earliest that I recall was given to my cousin. He comes from a family of mad-keen polo players but generally low on funds—a significant disadvantage in the glamorous, high-cost world of polo. Coached by his father, Julian showed considerable prowess for the sport from an early age. However, many counselled him against taking it up seriously because it would 'take just one bad fall' to put him out of action permanently. Instead, he was advised to take a 'safer' path along more traditional lines. Happily, my cousin, like many members of my contrary family, refused to follow that advice and instead set himself the task of completing his 'apprenticeship' as a professional polo player; he scraped together the funds the sport requires—aided and abetted by his ever-supportive parents.

Since then, Julian has achieved the equal-highest handicap rank for a polo player in the UK and now plays professionally around the world doing a job that he loves. Needless to say, ownership of his BOMOAG, his self-determination and the support of his parents led to his current success.

To sum up, the main benefit of fiercely owning your BOMOAG is that it makes you willing and determined to take responsibility for its successful accomplishment, despite the contrary influence of other factors and people. Although putting in the effort is easy in fair weather, it takes passionate ownership of a vision to stay on track in times of tempest.

Guidelines for goal setting

A ship in port is safe, but that's not what ships are built for.

Grace Murray Hopper

Psychologists talk about the importance of setting SMART goals—targets that are specific, measurable, achievable, realistic and time constrained. They ensure that not only do you have clear, appropriate and achievable targets, but you also have timelines by which to achieve them.

From building a house to baking a cake, the best processes follow a set of guidelines. Goal setting is a process, so in order to have the 'best', or most suitable, goals, you need to follow some basic goal-setting guidelines. David Liddy, CEO at the Bank of Queensland, says:

> I never want to be ordinary, so I never set goals that are ordinary. They need to be realistic, but also need to have some stretch

built in. I started with a company that closely resembled a Tigermoth with dodgy wingflaps. Four years later, we're more like a Boeing 737-800. I still have some strong stretch goals in front of me; I never want to run second, but I'm also really enjoying myself.

David was smart; he accumulated all the data he needed in order to set himself and his organisation some tough, but realistic goals. Archie Douglas, the founder and director of PRDnationwide, a well-known real estate agency, reflects similar sentiments:

Have a dream and talk to someone you trust and respect about it. Break it down into bite-sized pieces that are achievable, but also ensure that you have three-year stretch goals too. Aim higher rather than lower when you set them and say, 'I'm going to do it', Know what you have to do to achieve them and feel confident in yourself that you can.

Being specific when you set your goals means you can focus on what it really is you want to achieve. When you close your eyes, can you form a clear picture in your mind of finally reaching that target? Phil Hogan is specific in his description of his own goal-setting procedures:

I set different goals for different life aspects and for each life period. I also always write them down. In the first week back after the Christmas holidays, I list my different life aspects in order of priority. Then, I try to plan as much as possible including my life with my wife and children. I then write a personal mission statement for myself as well as a statement for each goal. I read that mission statement every morning.

Each morning, I also read the keys [included in appendix B] that I believe are vital to success. They're hanging on the bathroom wall. In my own space—usually the shower—I look at each item on the list one by one and contemplate each as it applied to my previous day and assess my performance. It then becomes a regular daily review.

Being measurable is equally essential. The indicator of assessing whether you are setting measurable goals is whether you are able to answer the question 'How will I know when it is achieved?' A classic example is of the athletes who — when asked what their targets are for the year — reply, 'I want to be harder'. Now, 'harder' is not a clear measure; it could mean improved performance on the bench press, or a marginal or significant improvement in an ability to defend, pass and run or greater mental toughness in the face of adversity. Few athletes are proficient at setting effective targets when they first enter elite-sport environments. Possessing measurable goals is usually one of the first lessons they learn.

Having an achievable target requires asking yourself the question, 'Do I have control over whether or not I can achieve this target?' Sometimes people have a bad habit of setting targets for themselves that are not fully within their domain of control. Therefore, whether you achieve your desired outcome is not solely within your control. For example, Olympic athletes who set their target as winning a gold medal are actually aiming for a goal that is beyond their control because part of reaching that target is dependent on the poorer performances of other athletes within the competition. John Roe, the Queensland Reds captain and an Australian Wallaby player, emphasises the necessity of 'stick[ing] to what's within your control'. In regard to his own goals as a rugby player, he says:

> I accepted I needed to develop as a rugby player, so my first goal was to play well enough to be considered for selection on the Queensland bench; then it was to start for Queensland; then it was to be on the Wallabies' bench; finally it was to start for the Wallabies.

Although selection is not within an athlete's control, John recognised that his own performances were within his control, and he could therefore maximise his selection chances. Possessing realistic targets is closely linked with having achievable targets. Not only does your target achievement need to be within your control, but it should also be realistic in terms of your skills, abilities and situation. Setting unrealistic targets positions you on an unerring path to disappointment. For example, I've witnessed athletes who set their hearts on playing in a particular tournament even though they had developed an injury. Realistically, they were never going to be fit enough to play in the tournament, but they still chose to aim for it. Consequently, they were left either bitterly disappointed due to missing it or, worse, they returned to the sport too early and re-injured themselves—leaving them out of action for longer.

Abraham Lincoln said, 'When you have an elephant by the hind leg and he is trying to run away, it's best to let him run'. It can be applied to the consequences of selecting unrealistic targets, which work in two ways. If your target is too easy, achievement brings little reward and appreciation, but if your target is too difficult, then failure will also result in disappointment. To combat this, David Liddy and Archie Douglas speak about 'stretch' being built into targets. Stretch is about the need to push yourself to achieve your target—to take yourself out of your comfort zone but to remain within your capability. That way, target achievement is imminently more satisfying, and it gives you the buzz of great self-efficacy.

David and Archie take the right approach—they amass the information they require before setting their stretch targets. They then conduct a 'reality check' on those targets by plotting out a reasonable pathway comprising smaller, process targets that are clearly mapped each step of the way.

The key to accurately assessing the realism of your targets is to gather information about your current situation and capabilities, and the resources at your disposal, before setting those targets. Additionally, if possible, gather information from those with experience on the pathway that is necessary to achieve your targets, before you set those targets in stone. Phil Hogan tells how this was relevant to him when he started in the investment game:

> I asked myself, 'Who's the best in the world at investing?' The only name had to be Warren Buffett. So I started reading all the information available on Buffett.

Phil also sought advice from other business people who had found sustained business success. This led to well-known private equity investor Leonard Green inviting Phil to the US to meet him. Phil gives the following account of their meeting:

> The biggest message that he gave me was to do your homework. If you want to be a successful investor, then get to know as much as possible about the company into which you'll be putting your money. If you have that information, you'll have a far more realistic idea about the degree of success that your investment is likely to have.

Phil's anecdote demonstrates that you should invest in your future in more ways than one—time as well as money, and plenty of effort. Take time to fully investigate your area of focus until you have sufficient information to make a call about the degree of realism of your target. Without that research, you're simply another blind punter. When I work with individuals on their particular goals, I tell them that we won't make any sort of decision on which direction they should take until an 'exploration platform' has been set up and sufficient data accumulated. After all, you wouldn't buy a house without checking it out first; BP wouldn't set up a multimillion-dollar oil platform without spending time on exploration; and Edmund Hillary wouldn't have simply woken one morning and said, 'What a marvellous day for a walk. I think I'll do Mount Everest'. It's exactly the same with your future pathway. Take the time required on your exploration platform to investigate and understand as much as possible about what you really want in order to make an informed decision about your targets.

Meeting milestones along the way

A BOMOAG is essential for knowing the general direction in which you wish to head. However, to maintain the wave of momentum you feel when first setting your BOMOAG, set smaller progress targets along the way. For example, when professional beach volleyballer Summer Lochowicz was training for the Athens Olympics, she set herself a number of progress targets along that four-year road of preparation. By setting and achieving those smaller goals, she felt regular fulfilment and validation throughout her journey—and was therefore receiving regular encouragement for her ongoing effort to achieve her long-term target. Of course, success breeds success—Summer went to the Games and represented her country in the sport she loves.

When I ask young rugby players who have just been accepted into the Reds Rugby College program what their rugby goals are for the next three months, their usual response is, 'I want to be fitter and stronger and a better player'. I promptly follow that up by saying, 'By how much?' In other words, those players—without specific, measurable targets—are simply moving forward with no particular end in sight. Do they want to drop five or ten points in their skinfold measurement or increase their throwing accuracy by 10 per cent? Bear in mind that psychologists do not set those targets; it is not within their area of expertise. Rather, they ensure that the athlete has, or will, set specific targets in consultation with a dietitian, trainer or coach.

Milestones are valuable in breaking up what might seem like an interminable distance to your BOMOAG. 'Milestones are vitally important in achieving your vision', says Jeff Miller, the former head coach of the Queensland Reds. Using an example from his career, he continues:

> With Rod Macqueen and the Wallabies leading into the 1999 Rugby World Cup, we broke the two-year period into three main sections, rather than having one long journey. By making milestones, our progress was far easier to track and brought closure to achievement, all by giving structure to our approach.

When you set your BOMOAG, make sure that if it's a long way off, you set yourself some milestone progress targets along the way. It will enable you to experience small successes that will help to keep your momentum flowing. Just as it's essential to own your BOMOAG, it's also equally important to own your milestones along the way. The easiest approach to setting up an effective pathway with progress targets is to draw up a continuum on a sheet of paper and visually plot out the key markers along the way. (For sporting athletes, those markers are usually in the form of seasonal training or competition elements; for corporate athletes, specific projects or project sections; and for students, points of assessment, such as presentations, assignments and exams.)

Next, for each of those markers, assign a particular progress target over which you have control and ownership. At this point, you may have to insert a couple of extra progress targets among the continuum markers—particularly if those markers are few and far between. Afterwards, sit back and take yourself through the pathway you've just mapped out; ensure that it is specific, measurable, achievable, realistic, time constrained and, most importantly, fully owned by you. Make changes where necessary, and then prepare to take the initial step on your pathway.

Trademark your uniqueness

What's the outstanding part of your game?

Scott Wisemantel

When you think about setting your BOMOAG or your milestones, consider the attributes that make you unique. Once you've identified those skills and characteristics, work on them to show that you offer something special. By consciously making your uniqueness a point of development, you will start to think of yourself as a marketable commodity. There is also a particular joy that comes from developing the 'outstanding part of your game'—any athlete will tell you that they love training in the areas in which they excel because it takes less effort for greater results. Australian Wallaby Drew Mitchell has similar advice:

> Look at things you're good at or renowned or remembered for. That might be a good attacking play or it might be speaking up in public. Make sure that those things aren't neglected when

you're working on your weaknesses. After all, those are the things that made you memorable in the first place.

Past Wallaby prop Ben Darwin reinforces Drew's comments below:

> Don't go against what you're good at. Find your most valuable skills and go with them. You'll end up doing what you love and being paid for it—and it's much easier. Identify those talents or particular strengths that make you unique and develop them.

The concept of developing your strengths is echoed by Dr Martin Seligman, proponent of the Positive Psychology movement. Seligman believes too much emphasis has been placed on rectifying weaknesses rather than on developing assets—resulting in less-than-robust success across workplaces and homes. By contrast, Positive Psychology advocates spending greater time focusing on personal assets and using those assets to enhance your levels of happiness and mental resilience.

You gain energy from using your strengths and engaging in activities you enjoy. You can then use that energy to develop your weaker areas. However, if you only ever focus on what you do poorly or where you are inadequate, you will have no energy to expend on self-improvement.

Always spend the greater part of your time on developing your assets, rather than on concentrating on your inabilities. For example, if you love engaging and developing others but struggle with accomplishing the minutiae in your day, structure your days so that you can spend more time in people environments. That way, you'll receive the energy to either complete the micro-tasks or develop a procedure that includes someone else tackling them instead. By focusing on what you can do—as opposed to what you can't—not only will it result in better performance, but will also result in increased happiness—a great achievement from all perspectives!

Knowing what sets you apart can also be your trademark. Former high performance manager for British Triathlon, Dr Graeme Maw, has this to say on sport-performance trademarks:

> The sport psychologist with the motorcycle racing team facilitated the discussions on a team charter. Basically, the question was asked: 'How do we do business?' They answered it with creating their own trademark that they had emblazoned onto all their shirts, 'FTY'—which stood for 'faster than you'. And that trademark uniqueness went for everyone from drivers to pit crew. In everything they did, the aim was to be the fastest and FTY became their trademark.

AnneMarie White was a media manager at the Athens Olympics in 2004. She set out with the aim of doing her job well, but also consciously made an effort to improve her workplace environment. She told me that on her arrival she was labelled the 'invader' because she was seen as an outsider. However, by her departure she had earned the title, 'Miss Sunshine'. She worked both on her strengths in journalism and her strengths in developing a strong people–work culture—and is remembered for it.

You're not limited to your naturally unique characteristics if you're happy to put in the effort to develop other areas of yourself.

When I work with senior managers, I ask them questions about their uniqueness. Questions include, 'What image do you want to put out?' and 'What words do you want people to use when they describe you?' Importantly, those answers subtly differ depending on the person.

Much of it comes down to encouraging others' expectations of you—take more control over what you wish others to see rather than leaving it to chance. It's also a marvellous tool to use for creating your image and impact.

People are unique in different ways—such as being talented technically or strategically, or in a management sense. Phil Hogan asserts the value of uniqueness:

> I want to be somebody different. I don't want to be above everybody, but I want to be unique. I want my children to be able to say, 'He was different'.

These unique aspects are usually pretty easy for people to identify and exhibit strongly. However, you may want to develop aspects of yourself to balance other characteristics. For example, you may identify that you want to be described as confident despite a natural tendency to show lower levels of confidence. In that case, the key would be to identify behaviours that would be described as 'confident'. They could include speaking up in a group environment that allows your opinion to be clearly stated, walking with a purposeful stride or sticking to your principles in the face of a challenge. You would then form a goal to execute those behaviours on a regular basis—even though the initial steps may only be small. As time passes and your efforts are maintained, you would start to view yourself as being confident—thereby drawing attention to the positive element of your image that you've consciously decided to make 'the outstanding part of your game'.

Thinking of yourself as a unique individual projecting a certain image right from the start of your interactions with people can be very, very smart. Everyone acknowledges the importance of first impressions. I remember my first impression of working with one of Australia's greatest ever swimmers, Grant Hackett. He was only sixteen years old when I first met with him. I was an adviser with the Queensland Academy of Sport's Athlete Career and Education Program; my role was to assist the athletes to balance various needs in their life and to plan and work towards activity other than sport. I clearly recall my interview with a very youthful Hackett, who was yet to really forge his mark on the world swimming stage. I gave him my contact details at the conclusion of the meeting and said to him, as I did with all athletes, 'If there's anything further I can help you with, please don't hesitate to give me a call'. His reply—as I was about to head out of the door—was, 'Thanks Miranda. And if I can ever do anything to help you, please let me know'. He said it with sincerity and respect. He is the only athlete among hundreds whom I have met who ever extended that offer. I have never forgotten it, and he stands in my mind as exceptional as both an athlete and an individual.

Years later at the Queensland Annual Sports Awards, I had the opportunity to meet him again. When I reminded him of the episode, he was as courteous as ever and laughed when I recalled his response. It is a pleasure to see him so successful in the pool, but it is equally heartening to see his success away from sport. Regardless of his sound swimming ability—an innate talent—there is nothing that can replace the practised skills of exceptional human interaction.

AnneMarie White tells a lovely anecdote about developing the image you wish to project:

> I was the only female on this particular board, and we were about to have our first board meeting. The coffee and cups were sitting on the table and everyone turned to me—in obvious anticipation for me to pour. Now, before walking into that meeting I'd consciously decided that I wanted to project a certain image of being on an equal footing and ready to stand up for my opinions. So it was that when all those faces were looking at me expectantly, I turned to them and said, 'So, who's going to pour the coffee?'

> It made all of them stop and think—and they were clearly surprised at my question—but it allowed me to make my position clear: I was not there to pour coffee and take notes, unless everyone else around that table was prepared to take on that role too. My approach worked. At the end of that meeting, we'd arranged for someone to bring cake to the next meeting, and for that one I declared that I was happy to be chief coffee pourer.

It may seem like such a little item to pay attention to, but the little things you do or say—from the start—will form an opinion in the minds of those around you about the type of person you are and the role you play. Be prepared to give and take with what you allow others to see of you, but look carefully at what that may entail beforehand.

Regardless of what you may like to think, first impressions are undeniably important. Moreover, you may never have another opportunity to rectify your original errors. In high-performance environments, that most certainly applies. Dean Benton, Performance Director at the Brisbane Broncos, always reminds me, 'You get just one chance with these blokes. Either you do it well from the start or you might as well simply pack your bags and leave'. It's good advice to heed and is another example of how conducting initial research and planning will pay off in dividends. If you know you're about to enter a high-performance environment, take the time beforehand to prepare yourself—learning about the people and the operations you'll encounter—and your efforts will be well rewarded.

Ultimately, be aware of the image you would like to project to others. Capitalise on a particular element that makes you unique—something that forms your 'contribution' to society, and for which you will be remembered. What is the legacy that you wish to leave in the minds of those with whom you make contact? It's all about being memorable for the right reasons.

Flat tyres make for slow journeys

Another theme that emerges when I speak to athletes about sacrifices and working towards their BOMOAG is their ability to balance all parts of their life. Aside from the necessity of instilling effective mental and physical recovery to combat any imbalance—which I discuss in greater detail later—human beings have more than one life area and should therefore have more than one life goal.

I mention earlier in the chapter that if you have difficulty securing your vision or BOMOAG, break down your life into separate areas and consider each one individually. The same process applies for achieving life balance. Start by drawing up a 'life wheel'. Shown in figure 1.1, a life wheel encourages you to look at each area of your life and set a goal for each one. The segment size of each life area should be proportionate to the approximate amount of time you choose to allocate to each one. As is apparent from the wheel, if one life area has no goal or if that goal is being neglected, then the wheel becomes inefficient because it shows a 'flat' in one section. In other words, even the smallest sections of the wheel need maintenance if the wheel is going to be as efficient as possible. It's clear from the life wheel in figure 1.1 that this person isn't spending any time with friends, socially. Complete absence of time with friends often indicates poor social support—therefore highlighting a need to develop this area.

Figure 1.1: a typical life wheel

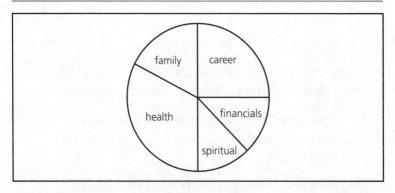

To further demonstrate how the life wheel can be applied in your life, example 1.1 depicts a hypothetical but typical interactive session between a client and me.

Example 1.1: the life wheel in session

Stephen is a forty-nine-year-old director of a small but highly profitable retail business. He has a young family

Example 1.1 *(cont'd)*: the life wheel in session

that includes two sons under the age of ten. A few months before he came to see me, he'd been told by his doctor to lose some weight. He tried a few different strategies to lose it, but they didn't work. Then one of his golfing friends—who had used perf-ormance coaching before—suggested that he come and see me to take a mental-performance approach to knocking off the kilos.

At his appointment, I ask Stephen to list his life areas —which he lists in no particular order as the following:

◻ home and family

◻ work and career

◻ social

◻ health and fitness

◻ financial

◻ spiritual.

Next I ask him what his goals are for each life area for the next six months. He outlines the following objectives:

◻ *home and family goals:* spend more quality time (at least an extra three hours per week) with his wife and children

◻ *work and career goals:* spend less time 'doing' business and more time (80 per cent) 'planning' for his business (strategic management and business development)

◻ *social goals:* attend his Saturday-morning golf games without using a golf cart to navigate the course (when he uses a golf cart he misses out on conversing with the golfers who walk the course)

▢ *health and fitness goals:* drop 15 kilograms and participate in the bike leg of the Noosa triathlon (after clearance from his doctor); receive a minimum of seven hours of sleep per night

▢ *financial goals:* put an investment plan in place for his children's future

▢ *spiritual goals:* increase his sense of inner calm.

To ascertain the amount of time he is spending on each life area, I ask Stephen to conduct a mental calculation of the approximate number of hours per week he allocates to each one. It reveals that out of the 168 hours in a week, he is allocating approximately fifty-six of those hours to sleep and seven hours to fitness. I then use the following sum to create a visual representation of how he spends his time in each life area:

$$\frac{\text{hours spent on the life area}}{\text{hours per week}} \times \text{degrees in a circle}$$

So when I calculate the time he spends sleeping, the sum is:

$$\frac{56}{168} \times 360° = 120°$$

Because the life wheel is the same size as a circle, at 360 degrees, the answer to the sum gives an indication of the size of the sector that represents sleep. (Note that it is not necessary to draw the life wheel itself. If your time-management skills are particularly honed, it may be sufficient to simply write in your weekly planner the approximate hours you spend in each life area.)

Despite Stephen coming to see me with the sole intention of losing weight, by looking at his life wheel, it enables him to build a 'life-sized' picture of where he wants to be;

Example 1.1 *(cont'd)*: the life wheel in session

it prompts him to focus on his whole life, rather than just a small sector of it (which can lead to the neglect of other life areas).

When we discuss why Stephen has been unsuccessful with his weight loss, we discover that much of his problem stems from his isolating himself from others due to his drive to lose weight. At meals, he eats different things to the rest of the family. Likewise, the time he spends exercising in the gym eats into his resting and family time, so he consequently resents going to the gym. In short,

Stephen has found himself neglecting other life areas in order to focus on what he believes he needs to do to lose weight; however, by doing so, Stephen has been unable to implement a routine that is likely to last or be successful.

On the other hand, by looking at the sectors that overlap in his life wheel, Stephen can now begin to achieve goals within several life areas simultaneously.

Rather than going to the gym, Stephen could shuffle his schedule around so that he rises earlier in the morning to go for a twenty-five-minute bike ride and organises for the whole family to walk together with the dog on Sunday afternoons. Not only would Stephen overcome his resentment of exercise, but he would also facilitate a healthy weekly activity for the family to undertake together.

Naturally, Stephen has a number of changes to make to his routine to meet all of his goals for each life area, but by drawing up his life wheel, it gives him a clear understanding of where he wants to be from a holistic perspective.

The lessons learned from the scenario in example 1.1 apply to you. By giving yourself a clear picture of each of the goals for each life area and the time you're spending on them, a life wheel provides you with a tool by which to measure the potential success of your various behavioural techniques. So if, for example, the time you're spending on your fitness regime is having a significant negative impact upon the achievement of your goals in another life area, such as your relationship, you're better off looking for an alternative approach to your fitness.

A challenge with the life wheel can arise when you are determining where to focus your energy at any given moment. It requires a keen understanding of your priorities at that point in time. For example, you may decide on a routine in which the first hour of your morning—say from 5.30 to 6.30—is devoted towards your goal of health and wellbeing. The bulk of your day may be primarily ascribed to time for work goals—whether they be related to your home or office. However, the evening may be the best time for your family-and-relationship goals. In other words, possessing a clear understanding of where to direct your energy at different times during the day enables you to be increasingly efficient with your resources.

Ponder points

» What is your purpose? What are the reasons for setting the goals you wish to set?

» What is your BOMOAG? What time have you allocated to achieve it?

» How are you continuing to remind yourself of your BOMOAG and your pathway to achieving it?

Ponder points (cont'd)

➤ Is your BOMOAG—and are your progress goals—really yours? Do you engage in behaviour because it's something you deeply want and believe in or is it due to the dictates of others? (Bear in mind that if you are doing it for the latter, your motivation will be harder to maintain.)

➤ Take all advice within the context of your personal situation.

➤ Have you ensured that your goal setting is SMART?

➤ Are you focused on and are you using your strengths? What is your trademark to performance?

➤ How would you like others to perceive you?

➤ Have you examined your life wheel and set goals for each life area?

Chapter 2

Where are you at now and what needs to be done?

Now that you've addressed the question, 'What am I aiming for?', closely examine where you're currently at on the pathway to achieving that goal. The clarification of that position is vital if you want to be accurate about the starting point from which to launch your plan for achievement.

Review and react

Aim for success, not perfection. Never give up your right to be wrong because then you will lose the ability to learn new things and move forward with your life.

Dr David D Burns

In sport, people talk about 'taking a baseline assessment'. It means that at the start of a team's preseason, each player is assessed on all components—physical, technical and mental—essential to achieving success. It provides players with a clear picture of their current strengths and areas for development.

It's exactly the same for corporate and life performance. You need to stop and take stock of all the components that are vital for you to achieve success. Ask yourself some questions: What's going well? What isn't? How far off am I from my BOMOAG for that life area?

It can sometimes help to draw a line from zero to ten, in which 'ten' represents 'goal achievement' and smaller targets positioned along the continuum represent the smaller target goals required to meet it. I call it a 'progress line'. It enables you to plot your current position on the line in relation to its perceived distance from your goal.

After you've created your progress line and plotted your starting point, return to it every time you review your success map and replot your progress towards goal achievement. Keep your progress line in full and regular view—some people like to use a small whiteboard and magnetic markers. Then repeat this technique for each life area on which you wish to focus your attention—so each life area should have its own progress line. It is a useful strategy because it provides you with a visual cue for plotting your progress—enabling you to use a visual stimulus that will reward and encourage you and help you to accurately determine how successful your efforts have been over each period of time. Example 2.1 uses the scenario depicted in chapter 1 to demonstrate the application of progress lines.

Example 2.1: progress lines

Return for a moment to Stephen's situation. After he's identified his goals, I ask him to draw up a six-month progress line for each of his life areas—showing his current progress status at the start of the line and his target progress status at the end. I suggest to him that he include smaller targets along his progress lines that will act as markers of his progress. He records the following:

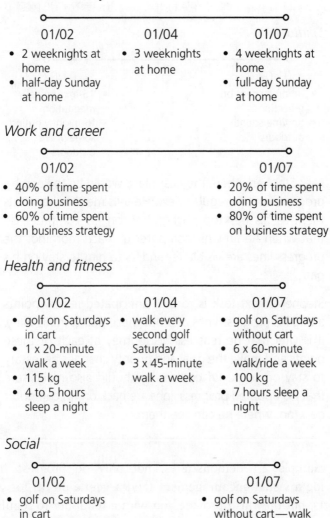

Home and family

01/02
- 2 weeknights at home
- half-day Sunday at home

01/04
- 3 weeknights at home

01/07
- 4 weeknights at home
- full-day Sunday at home

Work and career

01/02
- 40% of time spent doing business
- 60% of time spent on business strategy

01/07
- 20% of time spent doing business
- 80% of time spent on business strategy

Health and fitness

01/02
- golf on Saturdays in cart
- 1 x 20-minute walk a week
- 115 kg
- 4 to 5 hours sleep a night

01/04
- walk every second golf Saturday
- 3 x 45-minute walk a week

01/07
- golf on Saturdays without cart
- 6 x 60-minute walk/ride a week
- 100 kg
- 7 hours sleep a night

Social

01/02
- golf on Saturdays in cart

01/07
- golf on Saturdays without cart—walk around course

Example 2.1 *(cont'd)*: progress lines

Financial

○━━━━━━━━━━━━━━━━━━━━━━━━━━━━━━━━○

01/02	01/04	01/07
• no investment plan for kids	• decided on investment plan	• investment plan and regular deposits in place

Spiritual

○━━━━━━━━━━━━━━━━━━━━━━━━━━━━━━━━○

01/02	01/07
• no time spent on reflection • no time spent outdoors	• 15-minute daily meditation • fortnightly outing somewhere outdoors

I ask Stephen where the best place would be to keep his progress lines in regular view. He tells me that he wants them as his desktop background on his computer, so that when he fires his computer up each morning, the progress lines are visible reminders to him to stay on his path.

Stephen's next task is to plot anticipated review points along his progress lines and put those points in his diary. It is vital that he reassess his journey at each of these points and make the goal and priority changes necessary to stay on track. Of course, he should also make sure that his updated progress lines are back on his computer desktop, where he can see them.

As example 2.1 demonstrates, not only do progress lines provide a visual encouragement (and a gentle prod!) for your efforts, but they also provide you with a reminder to regularly review your progress.

Reviews help to determine the potential outcome of your success. They may include assessment of your past efforts and those of other people—who also influence outcomes. David Liddy describes a case in point about the Bank of Queensland:

> I made observations for the first nine days and then gave my first board presentation. Essentially, the organisation was inefficient; technically deficient and characterised by poor execution, and it lacked diversity—there were no women in the top four levels of management ... no urgency to understand problems and no sales awareness, and people were not a priority. I needed to make some dramatic changes if I was going to be successful in the role of CEO. That review then allowed me to understand what was required to change and to develop a plan to do so.

Likewise, Stu Livingstone, Strength and Conditioning Trainer for Queensland Rugby, is emphatic about the importance of the review process:

> Working with Eddie [Jones], he taught us to be very strong on reviews. We'd review and make changes while in the middle of a cycle of preparation. It allowed staff to reflect and make changes—we had to be flexible and adaptive. As information became available, we'd make the changes. That way, we weren't losing precious time. After all, there's no point in doing a review only at the end of the season, especially if you've been unsuccessful, because the time's already gone.
>
> I like to do a review and then record and set in place the process in order to action recommendations for when you're at the same cycle point in twelve months time. That way you're making changes to improve the present, but also giving yourself a head start on the program for twelve months' time.

Reviews also encourage you to continually refocus on your target. It's easy to become distracted by nonessentials and procrastinate or stumble over doubts about your ability to achieve the final target. Reviews consciously haul your brain back on track and—because reviews also make you stop and look at the real and achievable steps on the path to your ultimate goal—override your doubts (real or imagined) as you begin to see the road through the woods. CEO Rob Metcalfe has some strong opinions on revisiting goals:

> The more consciously we recognise, articulate and revisit the goal as being something to which we aim, we learn along the way what is the right thing to do. The goal becomes part of who you are and therefore simplifies everything you do—it helps decide what you don't want to do as well as what you do want to do.

In so saying, Rob highlights the effect of revisiting goals—that the targets and behaviours associated with it become an integral part of you. In turn, working towards those goals becomes less and less effort intensive as you increasingly exhibit those behaviours by default.

The review process also needs to be regular and consistent—regardless of whether performance is strong or poor. 'When things explode, examine the fallout and learn out of the failure, but even when things go well, continue to challenge yourself', suggests Archie Douglas. Reviewing your progress on the path towards your goals should follow a consistent pattern, so ask yourself the following:

- ▢ What is working well? Why? How do I ensure those conditions continue to be met?

- ▢ What is not working so well? Why? What do I need to put in place to overcome obstacles?

It's very common for teams and athletes to run a gamut of analysis and review sessions when their performance is unsatisfactory—but there is usually a degree of frenetic activity and a lack of clarity associated with doing so. Equally, when the performance has been strong, those review sessions often tend to be less than comprehensive—being accompanied by statements such as, 'Well, we won didn't we? There's no need to pull it apart if we did everything right'. By implementing a regular and continuous process of review that is factored into a timeline, good performances can be honed and poor performances can be assessed with far greater objectivity and less of a pervasive panic.

Assess from above

A life-review technique referred to as the 'fly over', or 'float over' (by people who want to slow it down futher), is a process that requires you to step outside your life and assess it from a more objective point of view. Some people may struggle with this particular review technique, but I know plenty of top performers from sport and business who find it a handy approach.

In a quiet moment—when there is a minimal chance of distraction—close your eyes and imagine you're flying over your life. Firstly, fly over your home. What do you see when you're looking down? Do you see somebody who is working on achieving the target he or she has set? Or do you see opportunities for behavioural improvement?

Now change your flight path and head out over your other life areas—work, social and health. Focus closely on each area. Do you see someone who is behaving in the best possible manner in order to achieve his or her target?

Make notes after each of your 'flights'. If your behaviours are below acceptable standards, ask yourself why that may be. Is the target inappropriate or are you lacking the motivation? Is the target too far away? Are you missing some key skills or knowledge to execute your target behaviours?

Flying over your life—although only metaphoric—can be entirely terrifying for some. One of my clients is a delightful and talented young volleyball player. She told me that she flatly refuses to 'float'. She wouldn't elaborate on why, but the topic of floating would often come up in conversation as an activity about which she felt uncomfortable. Imagine my surprise when in one phone conversation she casually remarked that she 'used to float a lot' when she was playing well and feeling strong about her performance and future. After further probing, she eventually admitted that she wasn't ready to float again because the prospect of facing her current situation and all its challenges was just too much. I now use the 'float' as a marker of her growth—I'll know that when she does choose to float again, we'll be making some progress on how she feels about her capability to tackle her demons.

Success breeds success

Before Alamein we never had a victory. After Alamein, we never had a defeat.

Winston Churchill

Reviews are also eminently useful for focusing your attention on successes and areas for development. Generally, human beings are chronically awful at remembering the things they've achieved; rather, their memories focus on the areas in which they've been unsuccessful.

By focusing your attention on your successes, you will not only remember what you have achieved in the past, but you will also probably be fired up with the belief that you can succeed in the future. I've heard some critics of teams say things like, 'They've forgotten how to win'. I would suggest that it's less about forgetting how to win, and more about forgetting that you are capable of winning. By disciplining your mind to focus on your successes, you're also forcing yourself to remember that you're capable of succeeding.

A time to plant and harvest

Your goals are usually closely integrated with what life stage you're in. At school, people follow a clear and structured pathway in which their lives are managed by rules and bells—external forces. But when people leave school, they are often faced with their first major decision—which is to consciously choose who it is they wish to be and what it is they wish to be doing. A number of transition periods are encountered by people through their lives—some are personal and others are career related.

John Reynolds, a frequent adviser to the University of Southern Queensland, conceptualises the potential career stages of a university graduate as the following:

1   *Backpack to briefcase* (at twenty-one years old). This
    is the transition made by the tertiary student into the
    workforce. There is a daily scheduling change as well
    as a change in focus. The initial weeks of working on a
    rigorous 8.30 am to 5.30 pm schedule can be
    exhausting for these individuals after coming from the
    comparative ease of a university schedule.

2   *Economy to business class* (at thirty years old). At this
    stage the intensity at work increases as levels of success
    bring levels of increased responsibility.

3   *Functional to holistic* (at forty years old). The focus
    changes from importance being placed solely on work
    to the benefits of working on achieving a balanced
    lifestyle.

4   *Executive to portfolio* (at fifty-eight years old). Once a
    balanced lifestyle has been achieved, success enables
    the development of a number of career interests rather
    than the person being limited to just one. Consultancy
    to a number of organisations and boards becomes a
    common practice at this stage.

5   *Plenty to offer* (at sixty years old and over). A wealth of
    experience across work and life can grant considerable
    objectivity and perspective at this stage, and that can

function as a resource in less formal situations. Time
away from the workplace facilitates the pursuit of
family, social and mentoring activities.

By understanding the nature of life and career stages as well
as recognising when change is imminent, people can learn
to anticipate the challenges of transition and develop tools to
match. Reynolds outlines a potential career-focused transition
program for university graduates that includes support and
assistance tailored to the needs of those transitioning from
backpack to briefcase. He feels strongly about the necessity of
educating students about the 'real world' and the importance of
work placements in industries that match their career plans. My
experience facilitating the growth of athletes and non-athletes
moving from tertiary study into work confirms that.

Networking skills and industry-knowledge acquisition are vital at
the *backpack to briefcase* stage. I always suggest to those about to
make the transition that they start with their close networks of family
and friends and then enquire about the people who are the helpful
contacts in those close networks. If you're at this stage, ask to meet
one connection over coffee at a convenient time and go armed with
some well-considered questions aimed at increasing your knowledge
of the industry and what it's looking for. Networking skills are just a
few helpful techniques that will help you navigate this stage.

But Reynolds's career stages aren't just useful for university
graduates; they are helpful for anyone wanting to develop clarity
on the types of support tools that are likely to come in useful.
Economy to business class is an intense period for career activities.
People in this stage require tools to help them develop effective
working practices to ensure other life areas are not significantly
neglected. If going through this stage, consider analysing
the systems and processes associated with your everyday
employment activities. For example, you may look at maximising
the effectiveness of your time management—such as by
implementing to do lists and introducing 'no contact' times during

the day in order to accomplish specific tasks without distractions. You may choose to finetune the communication channels in your team and those between you and the people you deal with—to ensure quality control of your product. (In other words, are you in regular and efficient contact with your team members?) You may also, for example, choose to upgrade the efficacy of your technical support, so that you can access the information you require to perform your role effectively wherever and whenever you need to.

Because this stage entails an intense focus on your career, often to the detriment of your other life areas, it's necessary to ensure that the rest of your life doesn't take a permanent turn for the worse. By introducing recovery periods—which don't include big nights out on the town—you will ensure that your energy is maintained for career output, and it will remind you that life is about more than your paid occupation.

As any elite athlete will tell you, to achieve success at a high level, there is a degree of sacrifice required. In order to be the best, athletes will sacrifice the time they would normally spend in other life areas to focus intently on their sport. However, successful athletes don't sacrifice effective recovery time or neglect their support networks. They maintain them for the simple reason that they know they derive energy from those areas—and that energy is vital for successful performance. It's no different for those aiming for elite corporate performance—neglect your recovery or support networks at your own risk.

So what about some ideas to address that potential neglect? For those in romantic partnerships, a good start is for them to discuss which evenings or weekends will constitute quality time together—and then to make those times as inflexible as medical appointments. For singles, scheduling time with friends or engaging in team activities is important. The *economy to business class* stage often coincides with the time when people are in serious relationships and considering starting a family, so the vital role of parenting needs to be integrated into the weekly schedules of these households as effectively as possible.

Because time is a premium resource during the *economy to business class* stage, when you're in that position, your emphasis should be on effective planning of your time. Apply the adage, 'Quality not quantity', to your time at work, home and play. Though a large percentage of your time is likely to be devoted to getting ahead in your career, ensure you're taking the initiative to replenish your energy stores through effective use of hours away from the office. Later sections in this book provide you with more on the concept of recovery, and a greater variety of suggested strategies.

Development of key strategies for those moving from *functional to holistic* tends to reflect tools to enhance the capacity for taking a macro approach to life management—the redistribution of time allocation to activities and the resetting of key goals. It can also require the management of destructive guilt that often arises with those who've spent long hours working and have developed the irrational belief that time spent on relaxation and recovery is time wasted.

Although this belief is less likely to occur if you've developed good recovery habits and energy-management systems earlier in your life, life at the *functional to holistic* stage should be about increasing the percentage of time and energy you spend on activities not related to your career. Unlike the *economy to business class* stage—which is characterised by a focus on career building and achievement within your field, the *functional to holistic* career stage is about reducing your intensity, broadening your priorities and increasing your development as a whole person, rather than predominantly as a 'corporate athlete'. Techniques you can implement to facilitate this include the re-evaluation of your BOMOAG and the targets across all your life areas, and the re-allocation of the time you spend in each life area. If you have children at school, this process may, for example, include the re-assignment of parenting responsibilities between you and your partner.

By contrast, the *executive to portfolio* career stage is characterised by diverse career interests as well as a balanced lifestyle. Here, you may consider your range of talents, your particular passions or interest areas, and then look at their application in a range of different situations. For example, you may choose to consult to different organisations or obtain positions—and still take the time to help out at your son's local rugby club or your daughter's sailing association.

When you're at the *plenty to offer* career stage, the focus is very much on being able to give back to the community. You have chosen to retire from your paid occupation and you therefore need to re-evaluate your BOMOAG and targets for each life area—and determine how you assign your time. Of exceptional importance at this stage is your perception of your value as a person.

After an athlete (whether paid or unpaid) retires from sport, because they've been defined by it for so long, they usually go through a period of adjustment that includes them examining their self-identity. Like those athletes, after retirement, many people find themselves asking who they are and what they have to offer. If you're at this stage, a useful skill to acquire is effective planning for the next stage in your life. What projects will you spend time on? How will your increased presence at home influence your relationship with your partner? It's vitally important at this point to refire your enthusiasm for the future and your engagement with life. Significant numbers of people over the age of sixty-five suffer from debilitating depression. So if you've just retired, to minimise your vulnerability to depressive symptoms, take the time to reset your goals and plan your pathway according to who and what is important to you.

So by ascertaining your position on your career pathway, you can refine your focus to develop key skills that are relevant to your current position. Now, I'm not saying that skill acquisition in general isn't a good thing, but when time is limited, a selective focus for maximum return is a handy approach—and Reynolds's framework provides that. This advice doesn't just relate to careers either; there are many paths in life and many types of transitions—such as those entailed when choosing to start a family, complete a trade, form a business, return to the workforce after an extended absence, live overseas, separate from a spouse and move house. All involve the challenges of coping with change and, frequently, emotional upheaval. Regardless of the path people choose, they will go through different stages in varying orders. The most vital thing for you to remember is that because everyone will go through transition periods, you need to recognise what stage you're in and when it is about to change.

Transition periods hold their own challenges—goals change, social and personal frameworks shift, financial and logistical issues can arise, and confusion about identity can appear. Who am I and who do I want to be? As mentioned earlier, transition is easier to manage if you make it voluntarily—if you take stock of your position, plan the way ahead and initiate the changes required. Resetting your goals then becomes vital for providing a direction in which to focus your energy.

I have clients who say they sometimes worry that 'life is passing them by' because of decisions they have made in the past. The key to managing those concerns is to have a clear awareness of when your 'scene changes'. For example, imagine a young woman who makes the decision to leave work and raise her children when she is twenty-five. She needs to be aware of when the influencing factors on her initial decision have altered—such as when her children start school and she has increased time on her hands as a result; she then faces different variables. In other words, the scene has changed and it now presents another opportunity for her to make a conscious decision about who it is she wishes to be and what it is she wishes to do.

The same can be said of those in professional employment. Say Ellen starts in a job because it was the 'best job at the time' and she has a mortgage to pay. Ellen needs to be conscious of when the scene changes—when she has built up her skills and experience to such a level that she no longer feels challenged by her responsibilities. She then faces another opportunity to re-evaluate her situation and make a conscious decision about her goals moving forward. On re-evaluation, Ellen may wish to continue with her current role, but at least her choice will be based on a clear and considered decision.

It is a common mistake for people to fail to recognise when the scene changes—when the reasons for making their original decision have changed or are no longer valid—and yet continue to do what it is they have always done because they haven't stopped to re-evaluate.

Putting it together

It's useful to be aware of your different life stages and understand the bigger picture of where you're currently at in your life journey. It's equally important to apply a beady eye to each of your life areas and identify your current situation for each—which is where progress lines can be helpful. Again, it's vital to assess each area based on your perceptions rather than on those of people around you—though feedback from others can be helpful to clarify your situation. (This is particularly applicable to issues related to work, whereby your performance is usually assessed using measures applied by someone else.)

So now it's over to you. Taking each life area individually and in no particular order, assess where you're sitting and plot an assessment on the progress line for that life area on a scale of one to ten.

Because you already set your BOMOAG for each life area in the previous chapter, you should find it relatively straightforward to plot your current position on the progress line for your:

▫ home and family

▫ health and wellbeing

▫ career

▫ social life

▫ finances

▫ spirituality

▫ other life areas.

How am I going to get there?

This is the most complex question to answer because it requires you to consider several influencing factors; if you fail to consider them, their presence can throw you offcourse. In an ideal world the resource of time is on your side—you would have the luxury of considering all factors and would therefore feel more confident about your final decision. Happily for sportspeople, this usually applies to 'start of season' performance planning, when they have the time to comprehensively and confidently assess their direction, current situation and the factors influencing their future.

However, most people don't receive that chance, and even for athletes, that window is only a small one—which is why sportspeople should take that opportunity while the going is relatively good. If athletes procrastinate about their performance-planning efforts, that window will close on them and they will be forced to compromise the thoroughness and speed of their deliberations. As the Romans said, 'Time flies'—which is even more true in today's hectic world.

In this time-poor century, a healthy mind is a fertile mind—and a fertile mind is far more likely to bear the fruits of success. In this section you will find some recovery strategies for maintaining great mind health. Implement recovery into your routine and you will be much more likely to reach your goals.

Recovery strategies

Adopt some of the strategies or use some of the tips and pointers within them.

▫ *Take time out.* Recognise the importance of down time as a tool for better future performance and current health. As George Gregan recommends, develop the ability to switch on and off to achieve balance in your life. 'Achieving balance is so important to me. Being away from work completely is rejuvenating—I can then return to training feeling refreshed and able to see all the positives in what we're doing'.

▫ *Plough the paddock; sow the seeds.* 'Thought stopping' is a technique athletes use to halt the flow of negative thoughts. It's a process akin to cultivation; you identify the weeds, rip them out and sow the seeds of positive thoughts—and if you don't, the weeds will grow back. Bear in mind, however, that those seeds (positive thoughts) need to mean something to you or the weeds (negative thoughts) will eventually overpower them.

Your seeds may be live-ualisations of you achieving your targets (a success crop) or live-ualisations of you being in your favourite place (a serenity crop). Develop your own set of key words or seed cards that will trigger your mind when it needs to be implanted with positive thoughts. For example, you may have made the decision to work on your fitness. You know that you tend to feel tired at the end of the day, but also that the period of time after you get home from work is also the best opportunity for you to take a walk.

So you decide that one of your seed words will be 'energise'. By doing that, the next time you arrive home from work and can feel your thoughts becoming negative—'I'm so tired. I just want to put my feet up'—you'll consciously be able to stop them and replace them with the positive thoughts and emotions attached to your seed word. It will result in you having your walking shoes on and heading out the door on that walk. Thought stopping enables you to be a firm but fair disciplinarian with your inner chat.

◻ *Develop support networks.* Every good paddock needs support from rain, sunshine and good fertilisation to help it prosper. Who is your support network? Who is there to help you flourish? Having your support team in place is a vital part of staying mentally well. Identify the people and places that pump up your energy and ensure that you're spending time around them—especially when you need to top up your energy.

◻ *Grow a worry tree.* Getting home at the end of the day is meant to be a signal for your mind to relax and switch off. Unfortunately, this can be difficult for many people. So try growing a 'worry tree'. On your way home from work, identify a point at which you will consciously leave your worries for the day. It doesn't even have to be a tree—it could be an inanimate object, like your front door or gate. When you reach your worry tree, stop and take time to consciously clear work-related concerns from your mind. Then turn your mind to thoughts of home or relaxation. Once you have those thoughts firmly in your mind, continue your journey home.

◻ *Write sunshine scripts.* When you're feeling completely uninspired, it's terribly difficult to see any ray of sunshine through the gloom—which is why it's a good idea to keep a few rays in an easily accessible pack. 'Sunshine scripts' are lists of your achievements, moments of intense happiness or times when you simply felt fabulous. Sunshine scripts enable you to 'rescript' some of the negative chat in your head by prompting you to recall the good things in life.

Start a 'sunshine book', which will enable you to keep a record of these energy-pumping moments when they happen. For some people, those moments include being made a job offer; for others, those instances include winning a hard-run race or the birth of their children. Make a point of reflecting on your day or week and then noting all the experiences that made you feel great on the inside. Then when the gloom hits, it's time to pull out the rays and absorb some sunny energy! I had a client recently tell me that putting her sunshine book together was quite emotional because she'd 'forgotten how wonderful those things had made [her] feel'.

▫ *Breathe oxygen.* Practise sitting or walking outside (preferably in a park, garden or beach) and taking in deep breaths of what the earth, trees and grass is giving you (oxygen). Then, as you exhale, imagine you're breathing out the 'black smoke' of your worries, doubts and stresses. Feel yourself being cleansed and renewed by nature. This is an easy and speedy exercise to do, and it can be used as the foundation for a number of activities—including meditation and live-ualisation.

▫ *Learn from the wise.* Inspirational prose and poetry can be both uplifting and used as a benchmark of your performance. My mother once told me to learn Rudyard Kipling's poem *If*. For me, Kipling was spot on with his accuracy—proving that my mother was wise to recommend it. I use it generally as a benchmark of my behaviour—as a set of standards to which I aspire. (Many athletes use inspirational and guiding material that is shorter and sharper, but no less potent.) Excerpts from biographies can also be similarly effective; for example, many people have been moved by cyclist Lance Armstrong's biography. Find something that works for you and incorporate it regularly into your day; make sure it's visible and that you frequently refer to it.

▫ *Say no to 'don't'.* If I said to you, 'Don't think about a large green apple', what image would come into your head? A large green apple, right? Likewise, if I said to you, 'Don't bugger up your presentation this morning', what would you see in your mind? A perfectly buggered-up presentation, right? This is because people's brains dislike and tend to ignore the word 'don't'. So it's better to have words in your head that reflect what you want to happen—not what you don't want to happen. Whether you're speaking to yourself or others, avoid the word 'don't'.

▫ *Undertake theming.* Pick a key word or phrase for the year or even just for the length of a certain task. (It could be as simple as, 'I feel strong!') Repeat the phrase or word firmly and loudly each morning and have it written down somewhere so you can use it as a reference point. The destructive words in your head can be so loud and persistent that it takes a loud verbal rebuff to shut them up. So if you keep saying the same positive thing to yourself for long enough, you will indeed come to believe it—despite any initial scepticism you might have had.

▫ *Exercise.* Exercise has a well-deserved reputation as an excellent recovery strategy. Aside from the obvious health benefits, exercise produces endorphins (naturally occurring 'happy drugs' in the body) and provides you with space to think, increased levels of energy, an opportunity for socialising and (for me and many dog walkers) great relationships with a beloved canine! Paul McLean, President of Australian Rugby and Director of FPD Savills, says he's an 'early morning person' who 'gets up at 5.30 every morning to do an hour of exercise'. Janine Shepherd is the same. She reveals, 'I need to exercise even when I'm down. I bike at home on the wind trainer with the radio on. After twenty minutes, I feel fantastic and could go on forever!' They're not alone. Eddie Jones, for example, goes to the gym every morning, and David Liddy takes a morning constitutional.

☐ *Forgive yourself.* 'Great services are not cancelled by one act or one single error', remarked Disraeli. Human beings are exceptionally capable of recalling all the disasters they've caused much more quickly than they can recall their successes. In fact, people remember their failures so efficiently that they can have a negative power that frequently cancels out the power of their achievements.

So you need to be aware of whether you are indeed attacking yourself pointlessly for your shortcomings. You also need to learn to forgive yourself. After all, do you expect everyone around you to be perfect? No? Then stop criticising yourself. Newsflash—you can't be a living miracle who does everything completely perfectly, so give yourself a break. Learn from your errors how not to repeat them, but then move on and use that knowledge to find success.

☐ *Meditate.* Many successful people—including Janine Shepherd, Rob Metcalfe, Roger Davis and Phil Hogan—extol the virtues of meditation. Many people meditate frequently and regularly.

Meditation is essentially about quietening your mind until you are able to discipline the direction of your thoughts clearly and without disruption. Meditation can be used to relax or energise, and it can be helpful for obtaining clarity and general wellness. It can also be used as a starting point from which to develop emotional discipline — or to undo emotional undiscipline. By regularly engaging in meditation, you're also regularly taking control of your thoughts and their direction — as opposed to allowing them to ramble willy-nilly. Rather than indulging in negative thoughts, meditation enables you to take control over those thoughts and send them in a far more productive and constructive direction. If you develop the habit of being able to manage those thoughts on a daily basis through meditation, you'll be far more efficient at dealing with challenges when trouble looms unexpectedly throughout the day.

- *Forward plan.* Tony Wilson believes his forward planning enables him to make effective use of both time and the power of music. He says that he uses music to 'manage' himself — by having 'three upbeat CDs' in his car to help him 'unwind' on his way home from work. He says, 'Just before I get out of the car for my last appointment, I make sure that the slow CD is cued to go for when I return'. He therefore wastes no time in switching his mind on to the path that he wants to focus on.

- *Be mindful.* This is a useful technique to employ — particularly if you're in the habit of spending far too much time worrying about the past and hypothesising about the future. Mindfulness is a tool that helps you to engage with your senses and appreciate what you experience. For example, the next time you sit down to eat at a restaurant, rather than wolfing it back in order to return to whatever it was you were dong earlier, take the time to savour each mouthful. Focus on the texture of each bite and the flavours on your tastebuds and think about the contrasting elements in your meal. Discipline your mind so that it focuses entirely on what you're eating. It will turn even an average meal into a fabulous one. It's also a brilliant technique for anyone wanting to lose weight because it slows down the eating process and makes you focus on whether you really want the food sitting in front of you. I've had clients tell me that when they start to eat mindfully, they realise that much of the junk food they've been consuming isn't even as tasty as they thought, so they independently decide to change their diets accordingly.

Also, there are times when it is appropriate to review the past and times when it is right to plan for the future, but mindfulness helps you live in the moment. For example, I use the time I spend walking my dogs for creative inspiration about the future; however, from time to time, I spend it in mindfulness—absorbing and experiencing the sights and sounds around me. Aside from giving my brain a break from work considerations, it becomes its own form of mental holiday because I begin noticing and appreciating the many things I usually ignore in my everyday life. Can I invite you to try the same?

❑ *Fire gaze.* Archie Douglas says he identifies well with this remark made by Allan Pease about the time spent by a typical male after work: 'After spearing the beast, we like to go home and fire gaze—not to multiskill but to focus on one thing and to be completely absorbed'. It could be that this strategy works for you too—perhaps you need quiet time alone that allows you to simply chill. Identify the location and time when you will do it and make it part of your routine.

However, do bear in mind that if you find fire gazing to be an effective recovery tool, ask others around you to be aware of your need and give you sufficient time and space to indulge in it. After your fire-gazing time has expired, you'll be available to help other people. The same principle applies to the parent who undertakes the balancing act of building a career while raising children. If you're a busy parent, there should be a set period of time when you can choose to be 'unavailable'—and it must be respected by the whole household. Ideally, it should occur at the same time each day, so it will automatically form a part of your routine.

The art of effective recovery is learned over time. Try out a few ideas before settling on a routine that works for you. Eddie Jones, for example, says that a must-have recovery experience for him is spending time in Japan each year.

Right, so now that you understand and agree on the complexity involved in deciding the 'how', the next chapter will provide you with an exposé on working through that complexity step by step—directing your attention to the three fundamental targets driving you to or away from your goals.

Ponder points

》 What life stage are you currently at?

》 What aspects of your current situation—those related to your success map—need consideration?

》 Can you identify your life areas? On what do you spend most of your time?

》 Where are you currently placed in relation to goal achievement for each of your life areas?

» Would it help you to plot out where you sit ona progress line and then use that progress line as a reminder?

» Put your progress lines somewhere visible, so they can both cue and reward your performance on the way to your BOMOAG for that life area.

» Have you included regular periods for reviewing and finetuning your success map?

Part II

Get set

Chapter 3

Internal drivers —
values and thoughts

Understanding your needs and wants is essential for effective goal setting. Whether that process entails an awareness of your BOMOAG or the behaviours that you must implement to achieve your BOMOAG, it's essential to have goals and behaviours that fulfil your needs and wants.

To comprehensively understand how you are going to reach your goals, you need to look at the three key forces that affect your performance—internal drivers (target one), external drivers (target two) and behaviour (target three). Start by closely analysing target one—the internal drivers that push your performance in a certain direction. Your internal drivers of behaviour are your values, thoughts, emotions and ability (knowledge and skills). Each of these drivers possesses the capability to alter or maintain your course of action. You just need to ensure that the direction you take is conducive to your end goal achievement.

Values

To master your future, you first need to master yourself.

Miranda Banks

Your values are the beliefs you hold that underpin your life. Those beliefs affect the decisions you make—usually at a subconscious level. Taking their values for granted, many people struggle to immediately list their values because they aren't aware of what they are. A simple way of identifying your values is to think about your wants and needs. What are the things that you feel comfortable about compromising, and what do you see as not negotiable? Wants are negotiable from time to time; needs are not. Your needs tend to derive directly from your values. By comparison, your wants are often associated with your values, but less directly. You can compromise on your wants from time to time—and it will irk you—but it won't make things unbearable like compromising on your needs will.

To cue some of your own reflections, here is a list of common wants and needs:

- a sense of contribution

- recognition of contribution—whether in the form of monetary income or verbal feedback

- the opportunity to be in a positive environment or have other positive employees and team members around

- trust and honesty

- autonomy

- challenging projects

- a chance to either collaborate or work in isolation

- clear expectations of one's role

- a career pathway

- an ability to see incremental progress

- possessing opportunities to see goals achieved

- an ability to have a work–life balance

- a feeling of pride in one's work

- a relaxed setting

- the opportunity to 'be oneself'.

Janine Shepherd, a motivational speaker and author, is a particularly inspirational person to talk to about overcoming adversity, but she also has some great points on doing things that make life that little bit more satisfying:

> We need to look at the big picture — at the fact that everything that happens in life sends us a particular message. But it's also about the little things too. I have the current luxury of being able to have a power nap from time to time. It's only for fifteen minutes, but it makes a big difference to my output.

One of Janine's significant needs is to have the opportunity to examine, understand and balance her spiritual side. She says she usually does this through meditation and energy-balancing exercises, which she sees as not negotiable for her wellbeing. However, by becoming a writer and speaker, she also fulfils her want of giving back to people and the universe. In other words, she could survive without meeting those wants, but achieving them makes life that much more fulfilling.

Like Janine, Paul McLean, President of Australian Rugby and Director of FPD Savills, is aware of a common need that is important to him — the need to have a positive influence and add value. He reveals:

> As Director, I facilitate the performance of others. In fact, last year two people whom I manage earned more money than me.

I thought that was great—I couldn't go to work if I couldn't have a positive impact on something.

Paul isn't alone in that regard; most people like to feel that they add value with their contribution—whether small or large. Barb Barkley, CEO of Womensport Queensland, expresses it as her 'need to do meaningful work—work that has a higher purpose', and says that she doesn't 'want to waste time'.

Roger Davis, Chair of the Rugby Union Players' Association (RUPA) and member of the Wallaby Alumni, lists his needs as integrity, reputation, health, friendship and humour in the workplace. When he first started out as chair of RUPA, he wanted to make a difference to the players already in the game. He says:

> You've got to sow the seeds for happiness and health when you're young. It's a short step for these players from 'Who's there?' to 'Who's that?' I want to pass onto them the importance of taking the opportunities that they have now—to 'grab the bounce' before the ball gets away from them. If I can't get that message through, then I'm probably not doing much good and there's not much point to my being here.

Speaking about the needs of his team, George Gregan refers to the team environment at the Brumbies:

> We need good facilities to start with. We also have to have a good understanding from everyone regarding the direction the team is heading to as well as a good understanding of each other. We need to respect others' individuality and that will make for a positive environment.

Moving on from sport, humour also appears to be a common need for those who have achieved significant success in their roles. Successful Australians, in particular, seem to have their own special brand of humour. For example, an Australian head chef gives this delightful list of rules by which to live:

First, never cook in suede or cashmere. You might think you can, but it never works. Second, never enter a nightclub with a name starting with 'nite'—it's such a mistake. Finally, when in doubt, add another egg.

But where do values originate? As mentioned earlier, your needs are derived from your values and beliefs, so you will usually need your friends, work colleagues or team mates to have similar values and beliefs. As a rule, values derive from your early experiences with adult role models and from your interpretation of other experiences throughout your life. For example, in the text below, Bennett King, the head coach of the West Indian cricket team acknowledges the influence of his parents on the values he holds:

> One of the things I value is consistency of standards. When I was working as a residential-care worker at a centre that received and assessed delinquent children, I was fresh out of uni, but I learned quickly that consistency was so important. It's now something that's essential to my approach as a coach. However, it's my parents who instilled in me the values of openness, honesty and loyalty. I think parents are the greatest role models—they have the greatest power to shape a person.

The values that shaped Bennett led to him bringing children from the assessment centre down to training 'so that they could learn what fun really should mean when you're only eleven years old'. So he played the role model to under-privileged children in the same way his parents were role models for him. Bennett laughs wryly though, when noting that 'it gives you a start when it suddenly occurs to you that Dad used to do whatever it is you've found yourself doing!'

Bennett certainly isn't alone in giving credit to the parental role. Barry Bull, an icon of Brisbane music retail talks about the importance of integrity and what it means to him:

> Integrity is about being true to yourself and the values that you've inherited from your parents. Just as I inherited trust, love

and loyalty from my parents, so I want to pass that onto my children.

However, you don't just learn your values—and therefore develop your needs—from your parents. As discussed earlier, your values are also shaped over time by your life experiences. Near-death experiences, for example, can profoundly affect people; many tell of acquiring a clearer perception on their priorities after a near-death experience. Likewise, when someone becomes a parent, it often results in the person becoming less egocentric as they begin to value their family's wellbeing.

Also, being exposed to different views, opinions and cultures over an extended period of time can shape your beliefs and what should be valued in life. Knowing this, Rob Metcalfe, when conducting corporate leadership training, gives his group an exercise referred to as a 'life journey'. Each participant is handed a large sheet of butcher's paper and pens, and then asked to draw a pictorial representation of his or her life to date—making particular reference to the significant, life-changing events within that chronology. Each participant is then asked to share his or her life journey with the group. It's a marvellous tool for gaining self-awareness about the events that shape the way you think and for giving those around you an insight into you.

Different needs for different life areas

You also possess different needs for your life areas, though they're generally linked to your values. For example, people's needs within their close relationships differ from their needs at work—even though their values about honesty and integrity may remain the same. When you've done your life wheel, make a note of the needs that you believe correspond to each wheel segment. The question of whether you are having your needs met will then be easy to answer. Answering that question will enable you to prioritise each need, but bear in mind that all your needs must be met for you to be truly happy and fulfilled.

Conflict between needs and behaviour

Meeting your needs is essential, so you must be aware of what they are and of the impact they have on your life. If you fail to meet your needs in a life area, you will struggle to find happiness and contentment in it. If you've set yourself a goal—whether it's your BOMOAG itself or the behaviour that you need to implement to reach it—that doesn't sit well with your needs, you'll have your work cut out trying to achieve it because you'll be working against your deeply held beliefs about what is important to you in life. Take, for example, the situation of a mother, Irma, who wants to provide her son, Josh, with the best of everything. Her BOMOAG is that Josh should always have the best education, holidays, toys and clothes. To achieve this, Irma has to work twelve hours a day, six days a week, and can therefore spend only very little time with her family. However, Irma has a set of values that includes the importance of quality family time and activities; in other words, she needs to spend time with her family to be content. Before long, aside from the obvious issue of fatigue, Irma starts to struggle with working long hours away from her family because that behaviour contravenes her values.

When you find yourself compromised like Irma, eventually, something will break—which usually leads to disaster on all fronts. The key to avoiding this breakdown is in identifying any conflict between your behaviour and needs early on and then re-evaluating your BOMOAG and tailoring your approach towards achieving it.

There are plenty of examples of conflict between behaviour and needs in sport—and they are often due to cultural clashes. One of the higher profile real-life examples of this was former ACT Brumbies rugby player Andrew Walker. An Aboriginal Australian and an outstanding athlete, Walker went 'walkabout' during a time that was highly stressful for him. Negotiating extended periods of absence in a professional training environment is usually difficult—much like most workplaces. However, Andrew was doing something that he needed—something derived from his Aboriginal culture and belief system—and it conflicted with the behaviours required of him to achieve his team's overall target. Something had to give and—because people rarely break their values—Andrew walked away at that point from professional rugby. Australian Rugby and the Rugby Union Players' Association (RUPA) have set up a program that looks at some of these cultural conflicts within the game and how they can best be resolved through understanding, education and compromise. Community consultation and representation of different cultural groups is a significant part of the process, but there nonetheless remains a chasm between the operating procedures of a multimillion-dollar organisation and the cultural needs of some individuals within it.

Example 3.1 demonstrates what can happen when your needs are not being met and your values are not being fulfilled in the workplace and explains how you can turn that around.

Example 3.1:
conflicting values in the workplace

Tom is the creative director for a top-end advertising agency. He's proud of his achievements, but he's starting to feel dissatisfied and uncomfortable and he's not sure why. He may just need a break from things for a bit or he may need to change workplaces. To rectify the situation, Tom needs to know what's important to him—what his needs are in his workplace. One of his needs is to feel that he is creating design projects 'at the coalface'. He explains it as:

> When I'm creating, I feel like I'm really alive! I'm using my brain for what it was designed to do. Ever since I was small, I've loved design—everything about it. It's a real buzz to think conceptually and then bring it all together and make it real.

In his role as creative director, Tom doesn't possess the opportunity to create on a regular basis because he's required to delegate to and oversee everyone else. He isn't able to do the designing himself, but is instead supposed to ensure it's done effectively before he presents the results to clients. Obviously, Tom's situation prevents him from meeting that particular need. Now Tom may have other needs that aren't being met, but for the sake of this example, assume that the only need that isn't being met for him is his having the opportunity to engage in creative work.

As Tom's performance coach, I ask him about his current situation. What could he change in his current role that would enable him to work creatively on a regular basis? Is his current role flexible in terms of the tasks he can undertake? If it is, then what would need to happen next in order for him to use that in a way that will help him meet his need? Facilitating job satisfaction may require him to present various approaches to his team and boss that ensure the key outcomes are maintained for his role while providing for regular creative work.

If Tom's current situation definitely does not allow him to extend his creativity, he should look at other ways by which he can meet his creative needs. One of those ways may be a complete role change — whether internal or external to his place of employment. Alternatively, it may involve developing a business area — in addition to his current role — that would engage his creative skills. (For many, what starts as a sideline task, often turns into a legitimate enterprise as needs are met and intelligent business management is implemented. More and more people are choosing to start their own businesses so that they can employ their skills in a way that they choose — thereby meeting their needs.)

Example 3.1 (cont'd):
conflicting values in the workplace

In those first couple of meetings with Tom, it's clear that he doesn't yet have sufficient information about his options to make a confident decision, so his next move is to spend time defining and exploring those options. Once he has sufficient knowledge about potential pathways for work that will meet his needs and engage him, he'll feel confident about making the necessary decisions and executing them. However, making decisions about his future must be based on whether or not he is able to meet his needs.

It's also clear from initial examination that his current role is not meeting one of his key needs—which is leading to his feelings of dissatisfaction. Something has to change and change soon or Tom's work quality is also likely to suffer.

It's not just for cultural-clash reasons that you may abandon your original BOMOAG or your methods for achieving it—feeling undervalued can also play a role. Like just about everyone else, athletes also need to feel valued. A common reason cited by up-and-coming rugby players for their moving between clubs is that they didn't feel 'valued' at their club of origin. Perhaps the head coach did not communicate effectively with them and ensure the players were confident regarding their standing within the squad. Unfortunately, this is not a rare occurrence in sport. Coaching resources are usually stretched tight and, as a consequence, the coaching staff often spend most of their time focusing on the immediate members of the 'run-on' side, and can neglect the more marginal members of the squad who crave the coach's feedback.

It's not about those players being 'soft' because 'they need their tyres pumped' before heading out to play or require 'a few words from the coach' about their performance. In fact, everyone responds well to encouragement and constructive feedback about his or her performance. Most acknowledge that they don't need others to tell them how brilliant they are on a daily basis, but every person with whom I've ever worked tells me that 'a little positive feedback goes a long way'. It's all about knowing your needs and, in particular, how you can feel valued for the work you do and ask for feedback on your value when necessary. Organisations, more often than not, believe no news is good news, so they only provide feedback to you — usually in the form of a visit to the boss's office — if you've made a shocking error. Even bosses are rarely given feedback about their performance in the top job unless they're performing below par.

So how can you ensure that you feel valued in your role? Start by developing an awareness of what your needs are and think about how you can have them met. Look at how that can be achieved within your current situation. Are you asking for feedback regularly and then demonstrating how you're using it? (There's nothing more frustrating than people failing to use the feedback given to them.) Do you have a mentor or good friend whose opinions you trust and who can give you honest opinions on your performance? Are you looking at your own performance regularly — identifying both the good and bad areas.

In other words, feedback doesn't always have to come from others if you're giving yourself accurate feedback. Self-feedback can't take the place of external feedback forever, however; it's important to identify someone who can provide objective and supportive information about your progress.

Meeting other needs

A need to feel valued by others in all life areas is common, but there are examples of other needs that are often found in workplaces, sport and at home. Example 3.2 (overleaf) demonstrates another need often found in the workplace — a need for autonomy.

Example 3.2: a need for autonomy

Lara loves her job. She's worked for the last six years in marketing for a prominent sporting association. Aside from initial training in the position, Lara has mostly had complete autonomy over her work. She's had great relationships with key managers and has found that she works best when given a project with a deadline and told to just 'get on with it'.

However, six months ago Lara's immediate manager was seconded to a different branch of the association and her old position was filled by someone else. Although Lara's new manager, Caroline, saw success in her previous position by working in very close communication with her team members, she did not gain much experience in dealing with senior management.

Lara finds herself becoming increasingly frustrated with Caroline's constant phone calls and demands on her time for meetings and 'updates' on progress. Lara feels undermined and undervalued. Despite loving her work, Lara considers making a move from the organisation because she can no longer cope with Caroline's management style.

It can be assumed that one of Lara's needs is to work autonomously. It's likely to be tied in with her belief that it's important to take full responsibility for one's actions and to take pride in one's work. Therefore, she prefers to execute projects without having someone constantly looking over her shoulder. In fact, because Lara assumes that Caroline thinks she can't cope with doing the work on her own, she is offended.

Two things need to happen from here. Firstly, Lara has to become aware of her need for autonomy. Secondly, she must communicate that need to Caroline — by conveying how Caroline's current behaviours are preventing her from feeling autonomous in the role. The following conversation is an example of how Lara could express herself effectively:

LARA: Caroline, I really need to talk to you about something important. [This flags the necessity of Caroline paying attention.]

CAROLINE: Sure, Lara. What's on your mind?

LARA: I don't know if you're aware of it, but when you called me for the third time today and we booked in a second meeting for the week, I honestly felt as though you think that I can't do this job without close supervision. [This refers to Caroline's specific behaviours and the impact that they have on Lara.]

CAROLINE: Actually, I think you're a very capable member of the department, Lara. I've just always worked closely with my team members and I like to know what everyone's doing — that way, I know how I can best help.

LARA: I really appreciate that feedback, Caroline. [This acknowledges positives.] But I suppose what I'm really saying is that I want to tell you what it is I need to work well and effectively. When I don't feel that I'm working autonomously, I'm just not happy. I understand that you have a need to understand what everyone's got on. Can we

> look at some way to meet in the middle—or at least another way of doing things differently from the way that we're doing them now? [This way Lara is being open to negotiation and acknowledging Caroline's position.]

CAROLINE: Sure. You must understand that I have certain obligations to fulfil, but I'm more than happy to sit down and work something out that's a better fit for you.

Granted, not all conversations—especially those with inexperienced or incompetent managers—run so smoothly. However, the example demonstrates that by being specific in your communication in the workplace—by defining the effect that certain behaviours have on you—and by demonstrating an openness to negotiation, you'll maximise the chances of receiving a positive response and having your needs met.

Thoughts

The next internal driver you need to examine is your thoughts. Are the inner voices in your head helping or hindering your journey to achievement? Barb Barkley reflects on the significance of inner voices:

> I suppose that the biggest start is that you have to get your internal communication right first. If you talk poorly to yourself, then you're going to react badly to situations. If you react badly, then you create distrust and bad feeling. If you then end up being fear driven, you'll only ever get part of the truth. You need to have honesty—trust situations and then the truth will flow.

Although Barb's statement is also relevant to how you talk to those around you, if you find you're beating yourself up when you get something wrong, you're attacking the only person who can get things right for you next time.

Be aware of what's being communicated inside your head. For example, your body may communicate to you that it's tired, but if you think to yourself, 'I'm so tired. I think I'll give the walk a miss this morning', you'll follow what that voice says and therefore miss out on your bout of exercise. If, on the other hand, you recognise that your body is tired, but you say to yourself, 'I know I'm feeling tired right now, but I also know that I'll feel better after going out and getting some air into me. I'm going to go for that walk', then you'll follow through on the plan you set.

It's the same for athletes. One of my clients was a strong swimmer and contender for state-level competition, but she always seemed to have an appalling meet at the national level. When we looked closely at her situation, we discovered that her self-talk at the national level was negative and therefore becoming a self-fulfilling prophesy of doom. In the lead-up to the competition, she would tell herself, 'The competition is scary. I never do well at nationals and I don't see why it's going to change'. Moreover, when she turned up for those swim meets, her inner voices would run rampant with gloom and predictions of disaster. She was setting herself up for a poor performance because that was what she focused on.

It's not hard to make a connection between sport and business. Whether you're anticipating the outcome of an interview, meeting or social interaction, if your inner chat puts your focus on disaster, then a disastrous result will be far more likely. Changing that rather nasty habit is challenging but not impossible. It takes awareness and practice. Be more aware of your inner chat — reflect on what's being said in your head. If the topics are terrible, then replace them with key statements such as, 'I shall do this well', 'I feel good about myself' and 'I want to sink my teeth into a good challenge'. Select a few key phrases ahead of time and make them a part of your usual routine.

Before embarking on a task, have your inner chat tell you that you're a champion and you're going to really do it well.

Developing positive self-talk is all about replacing bad habits with good ones.

Cognitive discipline

People tend to give their thoughts a pretty loose rein. So you may intend to focus on a certain topic—such as your monthly budget—but instead become distracted by other things, such as tonight's dinner, or whether you've fed the cat. In other words, your thoughts often operate in a gratuitous flow of undiscipline. To say that your thoughts have a mind of their own is usually not too far from the truth. Can you do anything about it? Because I'm a cognitive behavioural practitioner, my answer is, unhesitatingly, yes—but it takes practice.

To develop thought discipline, take a leaf out of the book of eastern philosophy. Meditation is, among other things, about consciously directing your thoughts in the way that you decide. So choose where your thoughts are going—rather than allowing them to form their own path. By practising some simple meditation techniques on a regular basis, you will begin to possess more control over your mind, and your overall ability to manage the direction and intensity of your thoughts will improve. Also, by linking a keyword to your meditative state, you will then have a tool to rapidly bring your thoughts back under your control.

Now, there are hundreds of ways to meditate, but below is a simple and effective approach. You should aim to meditate for only a short period to start with, and then work up to longer periods.

Breathe—focus—think

1 Settle yourself comfortably in a clear, positive environment.

2 Concentrate on your breathing. Take long, deep, rhythmic breaths without holding your breath at

any time. Introduce a keyword to accompany your breathing — popular selections are 'relax' or 'flow' and 'breathe'. As you exhale, concentrate on linking that word to the rhythm of your breathing. Repeat for ten inhalations.

3 Focus on a single point. It may be a leaf or a candle, for example. You should be completely absorbed by that point — everything else should feel blurred. Feel the connection between you and that point; for example, if you concentrate on a leaf, you may sense the oxygen emanating from it and feel the energy from it being drawn into your body as you inhale.

4 When you're totally absorbed, turn your thoughts to something specific that you've preselected — such as a problem that's been concerning you. Alternatively, you may want to simply 'fly over' certain parts of life because you want to go exploring.

5 If your thoughts begin to travel somewhere other than where they're supposed to go, use your keyword to bring your focus back to your breathing, and then go through the steps again.

As a postscript to these directions, be aware that when people first start meditation exercises, many struggle to maintain their focus even for short periods. If this happens to you, remember that it can be helpful to be guided by another voice. A good guided meditation CD can be used as a starting point. I also recommend that you get into the habit of meditating daily, even if just for a short time. If you do it at the same time each day, then you'll be more likely to embed the habit quickly. I like to do my exercises, for example, when I have my regular cup of tea in the morning.

Meditation is a marvellous technique for acquiring basic cognitive discipline. Not only is it beneficial as a relaxant, but by incorporating a keyword, you can also use that keyword when you feel your discipline is going AWOL. It enables you to centre your thoughts and then redirect them down the right path.

Believing in the how

Earlier in the book, the importance of owning your BOMOAG as well as the milestones along the way is discussed. The second part to ownership, however, is that you need to believe in the pathway by which you will achieve those targets. Most sports people will tell you what their goal is, and they will be just as convincing about their belief that they own that goal. The problems start when there is a lack of belief in the pathway—the 'how' that has been set for goal achievement.

Leaders have the job of convincing their teams that the pathway that has been set—either solely or collaboratively—is the best one for achieving a goal. Anyone in sport will tell you that sports coaching is one of the toughest industries, because not only do coaches generally sink or swim based on the outcome of their team, but the team's previous successes are quickly forgotten in the face of failure—and it often takes place in the full glare of public scrutiny. John Buchanan, the head coach for the Australian cricket team, is a case in point. Two years ago, he was touted as one of the most successful sports coaches in Australia. But after losing the Ashes series to the English cricket team, the media speculated that his job was seriously at risk. When John was criticised, it wasn't because the goals he'd set were wrong or were disowned by the team, but because his methods were seen as less than optimal. Again, there lay the connotation that the players did not believe in the pathway by which to achieve the goals and that the team was therefore unsuccessful. Happily, for Cricket Australia as well as the Australian sporting public, John retained his position as head coach and continues to build the success of his team and himself. His recent results—including the Australian cricket team bringing the Ashes urn back to Australia after losing the Ashes series the preceding year—speak for themselves.

I clearly remember a situation at Queensland Rugby in which a strength and conditioning coach with considerable status and expertise in professional sport was brought in to make an impact on the physical preparation of the team. For a number of reasons, the players did not believe in the philosophical approach the new coach brought to training. Their lack of belief resulted in less commitment from the players and, more importantly, lacklustre physical development — which was deemed a key reason for poor on-field performance that year. The lesson here is that if you don't believe in a method there's little chance it will succeed — regardless of its level of efficacy.

So, taking this principle beyond sport, if you don't honestly believe that attending university is the best path for you, you'll have a hard time completing your course. Similarly, if you distrust the person who gave you advice on how to advance within your company, you will be highly unlikely to follow those directions. Moreover, if you don't believe you have the skills or abilities to execute a certain task, you probably won't even attempt it let alone complete it.

If you want your pathway to target achievement to work, remember the following guidelines:

◻ You must believe that you have the ability to do it.

◻ You must believe that this is an effective method for achieving target success.

◻ You must trust and believe in the credibility of the person giving direction or advice, if your pathway is based on that advice.

◻ All the voices inside your head need to be speaking the same language as those beliefs.

Give yourself permission to perform well

People are not always particularly kind to themselves. They are perfectly capable of tying themselves up into knots of anxiety with premonitions of doom that, unfortunately, tend to be self-fulfilling. However, you can choose to give yourself the freedom to perform well. For example, Elton Flatley does this with his kicking. He reveals:

> My kicking coach, Ben Perkins, was great. To get me to play at my best, he would say, 'Give your body permission to kick the ball over'. So that's what I'd do. I'd breathe and then allow myself to get it right by focusing on getting it right.
>
> I use three cues for my kicking: nice and slow; head down; authority through the ball. I try to be in the zone when I kick, so don't think about it too much, but if I miss, then I use those three cues to bring me back on track.

Flatley concentrates on the specific processes that will most likely lead to a successful outcome. When he feels distracted, he uses those processes as signposts to bring him back to where he needs to be. Moreover, he gives himself the optimal chance of being successful by focusing on getting it right rather than worrying about getting it wrong.

The same lessons apply to life. Openly state that you will give yourself permission to succeed. Identify your challenges— anxieties and fears—and replace them with process signposts to keep you on track.

Live-ualisation

'If you can imagine something as if it's already happened then you're already most of the way there. It's about training your mind to attract the things that will make it happen, that you need in order to achieve it', says Janine Shepherd. This method is particularly helpful for her book writing, but she also uses it in other parts of her life.

Janine's advice demonstrates that to truly believe in the pathway that leads to your goal, it helps to envisage yourself as reaching that desired outcome. Visualisation is a technique that involves 'seeing' something specific in your mind. It's underscored by the principle that if you can see what you want to happen frequently enough, you'll be able to convince your brain that your objective is not only within the realms of possibility, but that it is also the most likely outcome.

'Live-ualisation' is a similar technique to visualisation — in that it involves visualising success; however, live-ualisation adds to the intensity of what you can see in your mind. For example, if you have set yourself the target of exuding confidence in meetings, practise 'seeing' what that would look like but make it specific. What room are you in? Who else is there? What are you touching, wearing, smelling, hearing or even tasting? The principle behind effective live-ualisation is that you 'live' an image in your head so vividly that your body reacts as though it actually happened.

The most extreme comparison I can give to live-ualisation is the nightmare. People who have ever had a nightmare will speak of its apparent reality — indeed, the human body will physically react to a nightmare, despite the fact that the experience is not real. If you use all of your senses to vividly create what you want to happen, you'll create a map in your mind of what you want and how to get there. Your mind will believe that it's already reached your goal and therefore be convinced that success is not only possible, but also eminently achievable. It's essential that once you've mastered some clarity of vision in the live-ualisation exercise, you undertake regular practice — at least once a day. In addition, ensure that your live-ualisation occurs in real time; in other words, don't close your eyes for a nanosecond and assume that gives you the time to visualise your desired outcome. Take the same amount of time when you live-ualise as you would if the situation was real.

Once mastered, live-ualisation has a multitude of uses — including the following:

- Use live-ualisation to 'set' your brain for the day. Take a moment before settling into your routine for the day to mentally 'see' yourself as doing things successfully, positively and energetically.

- Increase your arousal levels by live-ualising something exciting—something that pumps up your adrenalin.

- Decrease your arousal levels by live-ualising a quiet or favourite place where you feel at ease.

- Give yourself a 'self-confidence power bar' by live-ualising your most prominent successes. Take yourself back to that moment of achievement and relive it, step by step, in real time.

- Study the opposition and prepare yourself to do it better than them.

- Use live-ualisation to take yourself through a confrontation with the opposition. Live out what their behaviours and your responses are likely to be and repeat for a number of possible scenarios.

- Use live-ualisation to map out possible future pathways. By anticipating challenges, you'll be able to formulate the best way to meet them.

Mental blocks

You can't solve a problem with the same mind that created it.

Albert Einstein

You know the feeling—you've been sitting and staring at a problem for the last ten minutes—but it feels like ten hours. Not only do you have a complete mental block about how to deal with it, but your frustration levels are threatening to blow a circuit in your brain. If you sit there for much longer, you're more likely to explode than come up with the answer.

There are a couple of things at work here. First, your thinking is stuck in a rut — it's become focused on a very narrow path that isn't the right one. Second, the arousal levels in your brain are too high to allow anything else to distract you from that direction of thought.

To expand the horizons of your thinking, you need to be both distracted and relaxed. Take a physical and mental break. To drop your arousal levels, don't head for the nearest caffeine provider. Instead, go for a stroll, or talk to a friend, colleague or even a pot plant nearby. Think about happy topics — such as holidays, raucous dinner parties or football practice with your kids.

When you're feeling somewhat refreshed and a little more relaxed, return to the problem, but this time take a more creative approach. Look closely at the task. What are its attributes? What are its opportunities? Fully nut out all information about the problem before you start brainstorming possible solutions. In fact, if you can, ask for some input from others to gain another perspective. Finally, select the best-fit solution. For example, Dean Benton, Performance Director for the Brisbane Broncos, believes that 'if time permits, sleep on it and the answer always comes in the morning'. He says he uses that philosophy whenever he has a particularly difficult problem and the luxury of time. He talks here about a specific problem-solving challenge he faced:

> Motivating people to do what you want is a key part of my role, so I need to work out what the catalyst is for them. Just recently, I had a particular athlete and I had a lot of difficulty with him. He didn't really want to do the work and wasn't making weight. I'd tried a number of options with him — including fining systems and increased exercise punishment (the latter isn't a preference as I believe that exercise is a privilege). So I slept on it. In the morning, I sat back and looked at him as an individual. On reflection, I realised that he had no concept of the value of money, so fines didn't work. He also wasn't bothered by additional exercise requirements. But his great love was playing

the game on the weekends. To push his buttons, I'd need to deprive him of that opportunity to play ... To date, it's been very effective.

Dean's story is an example of effective problem-solving—he stepped back from the problem, relaxed his mind and returned with a different approach. He didn't immediately look for a solution, but instead examined the nature of the challenge. Once he identified what made the player tick, he could tailor and implement a far more effective motivational device.

The key to effective problem-solving is to acquire the right mindset. If you are stuck in the wrong mindset and too frustrated to let other solutions in, then you won't find success. Start with an open and fertile mind—gauging the characteristics of the problem—and then devise and test possible solutions before finding the best fit.

Champion mindsets

Human beings, by changing the inner attitudes of their minds, can change the outer aspects of their lives.

Henry James

There are many books about the impact of life-changing events. These events are often traumatic or dangerous and you wouldn't wish them on your worst enemy. From battling illness to overcoming terrifying accidents, these stories describe dark days that none would wish to emulate.

However, can you circumvent the negative effects of a traumatic experience by adopting a new approach to life? Absolutely, but it takes effort. You need to crank up your awareness of how you currently tackle life; consciously choose to exclude the elements that are negative and develop those that are positive.

It's equally important to practise the default elements you want to revert to in times of intense pressure, so that you'll automatically present that behaviour in difficult times. Performing under pressure is a great example of how those processes stand up. Many people need to act under pressure frequently — and it is usually the result of the perceived importance of the consequences of those actions or time limitations.

When people have to operate under that pressure in an unfamiliar or uncomfortable environment, the stress they feel becomes intense — as those athletes who've ever competed in an away game will tell you.

Drew Mitchell can attest to the pressure felt by sports people in unfamiliar environments. Due to a number of injuries affecting some key players in the Australian Wallabies, he received the call-up to play in a Bledisloe Cup game in Sydney. He recalls:

> In the media, it seemed as though every All Black player was saying that they were going to really target me — threaten me with high balls. This was the biggest game of my career to date and it was pretty daunting to hear that stuff. I was lucky because everyone in our squad told me to back myself, but essentially my decision about how I was going to approach the game came down to me. I decided to front-foot them and meet their challenges with confidence. I was so nervous that I was even throwing up on field, but my plan was to get on top of them early, so that's what I did.
>
> I've used that experience to build my confidence up from there. I figure that if I've played at that level, I can take on anyone regardless of the colour of their jersey because I've played them before.

Drew makes the point that under pressure his approach is to anticipate the opposition's moves and act before them based on that information. After all, blanket directives such as, 'Beat them before they beat you' are too generic to be useful. Likewise, have you ever improved your performance after hearing bland instructions such as, 'Well, you just have to be better'? In pressure situations, the key is to know exactly what to do next—as explained by Drew below:

> Now, I break the game down. We have a game plan for the team that's talked about in the lead up to the game. Then, for me, I size up people in the first five minutes. I look at how they operate and pick them early. I look at their areas of strength or weakness and how I can beat them. By breaking it down, I get to see how I can get them and it gives me that added confidence.

Drew's story highlights the value of choosing your mindset before the event and being clear on the steps you're going to take when the pressure is on. Your mindset will determine your actions when you're under the pump. Your confidence—a key contributor to your mindset—will come from knowing what to do next in a situation.

Professional Australian Rugby Union (ARU) referee Scott Young describes his work as people management. He recalls one particular decision he had to make under some extraordinarily intense pressure that illustrates the importance of following a preconsidered decision-making process:

> It was a match in Buenos Aires—Argentina against New Zealand. [There were] 75 000 Argies [Argentine players] in River Plate Stadium and Maradona on the sidelines. You could feel the ground vibrate every time the crowd rose up. The game was going reasonably well until the Argentine captain—who's also a half-back—decided to headbutt one of the Kiwis. The touch judge comes up to speak to me and I know that it's either a case of the red card [sent off for the match] or yellow card [ten minutes on the sideline].
>
> In a matter of seconds I had to weigh up a number of factors: first, the current Argentine atmosphere was hairy—they'd gone through four presidents in five months and looting was still rife, causing turmoil throughout the country; second, with the Argentine fiery culture and the vibe of the 75 000-strong crowd, there was likely to be a free-for-all if I sent off their very

high-profile captain; third, Maradona was on the sidelines and likely to raise hell, even if nobody else did. Actually, I heard afterwards that even the commentator said that this situation was going to cause trouble if I sent the captain off for the match. So taking as much of the emotion out of the situation as possible, in a calm delivery, I sent the Argentine captain to the sin bin.

I believe that I made the right decision at that time because I'd trained myself to identify sequences of behaviour and respond to them according to set processes that I'd had in place — just as a CEO would with any volatile situation. The other strong reinforcement for that decision was external — both Argentine players and New Zealand players came up to me after the game and said that the situation had been managed well.

One of the key areas for team training is practising performance under pressure, particularly with regard to decision making. Fabricating pressure can be difficult without the obvious accessories of noisy crowd and importance of game outcome, so coaches will often create pressure by applying time limitations. By doing this yourself, you too can hone your performances under high-pressure conditions. The more you practise under those conditions, the more effective you'll be when the pressure is real.

So when somebody next asks you for action, take confidence in making your decision, rather than leaving it up to them. Champions don't just wait for the championship to facilitate clear decision making; they consciously practise it every day.

Ponder points

⏩ What are your wants and needs? Make a list of those that are relevant to each of your life areas.

⏩ Reflect on your values. Where did they come from?

Ponder points (cont'd)

➡ Having worked out the direction in which you want to head and fixed your sights on your BOMAOG, you now need to ask yourself the question, 'Do I currently have what it takes to achieve it?'

➡ Are your thoughts aligned to believing in your path and capabilities or are they being destructive and telling you otherwise?

➡ What are your inner voices telling you?

➡ Is the language that you're using reflective of success or failure?

Chapter 4

Internal drivers — emotions and ability

Of course, your values and thoughts are not the only internal drivers of your behaviour and performance; your emotions and your ability also drive you in a certain direction. This chapter provides you with suggestions for ways to manage your emotions and arousal levels so you can better reach your goals, and it explores the role that skills and knowledge plays in achieving your aims.

Emotional discipline

He that is slow to anger is better than the mighty; and he that ruleth his spirit is better than he that taketh a city.

Proverbs 16:32

Closely linked with your thoughts are your emotions. Emotions are simply the umbrella term for what you're feeling. Negative emotions generally lead to destructive thoughts, which can in turn lead to more negative emotions. By contrast, positive emotions generally lead to happy, constructive thoughts, which result in more positive emotions.

Intuitively, this makes sense—negative thoughts feed into and out of negative emotions and positive thoughts feed into and out of positive emotions. How is this relevant to performance though? Do negative emotions automatically mean poor performance? Interestingly enough, the answer is no.

Research into emotions and performance has indicated that, at times, negative emotions—such as anxiety, anger and antipathy towards the competition—are key components of an 'ideal' performance. Yuri Hanin developed the Individual Zone of Optimal Functioning theory in the late 1980s based on the premise that different athletes produce best performances at different levels of anxiety. Hanin believes some athletes require low levels of the negative emotion of anxiety for top performances while other athletes require higher levels of anxiety to perform well. Research over the last twenty years has built on this theory and found that other so called negative emotions—such as anger—are necessary for some athletes wanting to facilitate top performances.

Although it sounds initially counter-intuitive, these results make sense in practice. Athletes often tell how their frustrations—such as at being evaluated poorly by their coach—result in improved performance because they want to 'show the coach' that he or she 'was wrong'. Equally, a degree of nerves can metamorphose into energy for on-court brilliance.

One of the underlying principles of theories about the influence of emotions on performance is that it's important how individuals interpret their emotions. So if you're lining up to give a presentation to the board one morning, you may feel nervous, excited, frustrated or relaxed. However, it's not the emotions that you're experiencing that are likely to influence your performance, but, rather, how you interpret those emotions and the degree to which you feel them. In other words, if you score yourself a seven out of ten for nervousness and believe that to be a dreadful situation—particularly because you felt this nervous the last time you presented and it ruined your presentation—your performance is likely to be negatively affected. On the other hand, if you interpret your level of nervousness as being more exciting than dire, your performance is likely to be influenced positively.

By contrast, if your level of nervousness is low, you may be concerned that you're feeling relaxed to the point of saying, 'Whatever'—leading to a below-par performance. Alternatively, you may feel that you do your best work when you're relaxed—thereby maximising the positive effect it has on your upcoming performance. The key points here are the following:

□ An awareness of your emotions and how you interpret them is of crucial importance.

□ When you've identified what you're feeling and what you think about it, you need to know what to do about it; in other words, be aware of what needs to change about how you manage your emotions so that you can maximise successful performances.

In order for you to manage your emotions effectively, you must undertake the following steps:

1 Think back to certain situations you've been in. You might have categorised them as groups of experiences under headings such as 'presentations and sales', 'planning and creativity', 'management', 'family meetings' or 'fitness training'.

2 Next, group together under each heading your 'best' performances and your 'worst' performances

3 For each of your 'best' examples, think back and recall the emotions you experienced (both positive and negative) just

before executing your performance. List them, including the approximate level of intensity (use a scale of one to ten) that you believe you experienced for each emotion.

4   Repeat that procedure for each of your 'worst' examples.

By doing those steps you will have created two separate emotional profiles for each situational group. For example, if you have an emotional profile for successful performance for presentations and sales, the next time you make a presentation, you'll know that you need to aim for an approximate level of anxiety if you want to nail a good performance.

Your emotional profiles for 'worst' performances provide you with information about emotions not to experience — in other words, if you're experiencing them, then you know you need to do something about it to improve performance outcomes. By following those steps, you will have approximate targets for the 'ideal' emotions needed to facilitate your best performances across a range of situations.

The next step is to increase your awareness of what you're feeling prior to key performances and to enlist the assistance of 'tools' to increase or decrease the presence of certain emotions.

Emotional discipline is the skill of being able to manage your emotions; it's about starting off in the direction you want to head in, being aware of when you're lost and knowing how to get back on track when you veer offcourse. The principle to bear in mind is that by managing your emotions successfully, you're consciously directing your limited energy sources towards where they can be best used.

You only have a limited amount of energy, and if it's not focused, it will be wasted. Too often do people allow their emotions a free rein — which leads to the dissipation of their already limited energy stores. So whether in a position of leadership over others or not, you should always take a position of leadership over yourself and your emotions if you want to maximise your energy output.

Managing yourself is not always an easy task. Athletes, for example, are often forced to manage their emotions in public forums. Reflect on media interviews conducted with captains of winning teams; think of the jubilation, happiness, relief and the 'We showed you all' attitude clearly on display. Contrast this with interviews done with the captains of losing teams; you clearly see their disappointment, frustration and sometimes downright humiliation depicted in public.

To assist athletes to manage those stressful situations, they're given training and a clear structure on how to answer questions. They're given the opportunity to consider situations in advance and plan and practise their approach in order to manage their emotions.

Emotional management requires changing how you usually operate, so it's therefore effort intensive. If you're going to be successful at controlling your emotions, you really need to want to change.

For example, a rugby player came to see me because he wanted to get a handle on how he could better manage himself on field. He had what I call the 'battle fugue' — while playing he'd exhibit completely out-of-control anger levels and want to wallop the closest member of the opposition. Knowing how hard it can be to rein in the 'beast of anger', I asked him why he really wanted to change. His answer — which I've never forgotten — was:

> It's about the little kids on the bus — those little kids come along with Dad or Mum to watch us play. I remember being a little kid on the bus once, coming in to watch my heroes play too. The last thing I want is for one of those kids to see me losing it out there on field. What sort of example does that set?

Funnily enough, something in his response proved to be the best deterrent for his behaviour; he wrote the word 'bus' on the strapping around his wrist. If he started to feel that he was 'losing it' on field, he'd just look down and remind himself of what else he was doing out there—setting an example. It worked a treat. Although he was never the captain of a state side, he was a natural leader—and there were plenty who could have learned from his example. More importantly, for his behaviour-change strategies to be successful, he had to really want to change—and he did.

Tools for emotional discipline

Emotions influence your performance by changing your thoughts and behaviours. Your capacity to focus is altered by the effects of different emotions—for example, you probably tend to focus better while feeling confident, happy and prepared for a challenge.

Groups of emotions interacting together influence your arousal levels. Though the word 'arousal' is enough to send titters of self-conscious laughter through my first- and second-year psychology students at university, it is used in sport to refer to a more generic circumstance—the degree to which a person is 'psyched up' or emotionally energised about a particular task.

Although predominantly influenced by anxiety, your arousal may be influenced by any or all emotions to some extent. Most importantly, however, your arousal levels directly affect your performance.

Once you understand that emotions interact in a way that significantly influences your arousal, it enables you to develop tools and strategies to manage your arousal—which in turn helps you to manage your emotions and influence your performance.

There are many tools that you can use to replace or modify your emotions. For example, the rugby player who had trouble controlling his anger negated his experience of intense 'battle' anger by being aware of the responsibility that comes with being a role model. You possess techniques that enable you to exert influence over your emotions—you just need to tap into those tool. Table 4.1 includes strategies—some taken straight from athletes—for increasing or decreasing the effect that your emotions have on you.

Table 4.1: emotional-management techniques

Emotion	Increase effect	Decrease effect
Happiness	• Recall three memories of happy events—for example, your dogs playing with a bone or you playing cricket with your children • Think of future success	• Recall three memories of sad events • Think of future failures
Anxiety	• Live-ualise yourself making a mistake • Think about how important an upcoming performance is to you • Worry about what others think	• Live-ualise yourself experiencing success • Say things to yourself like, 'I can do this!' or 'I have control over my destiny' • Remember that you have people around you to support you and back you up
Anger	• Remember when someone treated you badly • Remember when someone treated your family badly • Be defiant and say, 'No-one messes with me'	• Refocus your attention on another topic • Think about what you have to do and how to do it • Breathe deeply

Table 4.1 *(cont'd)*: emotional-management techniques

Emotion	Increase effect	Decrease effect
Anger *(cont'd)*		• Remove yourself from the source of your anger
Feeling 'in the zone'	• Develop a narrow line of vision—so that everything outside your focus is blurred • Use a key word to orient yourself • Minimise distractions • Set yourself a specific timeframe for that focus	• Think about people and places that are removed from your current situation • Look away from your current situation and broaden your view • Switch to 'explore' mode from 'analyse' mode • Set alarms to distract you and change your focus
Competitiveness	• Recall the feeling of winning • Live-ualise moments of being toe-to-toe with your opponent • Live-ualise being beaten when you don't want to be	• Think about the process instead of the outcome—recall what needs to be done in order to win, rather than the win itself • Compare yourself to your markers of progress—not other people's

Emotion	Increase effect	Decrease effect
	• Revel in your confidence as a strong competitor	• Increase your feelings of relaxation
Feeling energised	• Say things to yourself that reflect great internal energy—like, 'I have springs in my feet!' • Go for a brisk walk for a few minutes • Live-ualise moments when you've felt very energised before	• Think to yourself, 'I'm feeling very tired' • Listen to calming music • Take warm baths and practise aromatherapy • Slow down your breathing and try to imagine that you feel very heavy and relaxed • Use a keyword —for example, 'calm' or 'slow' • Listen to rhythmic sounds—such as waves at the beach

Bear in mind that, most of the time, you won't want to spend a whole lot of time increasing your negative emotions. However, as earlier mentioned, there may be moments when the presence of certain negative emotions may help your performances. Knowing how to manipulate your emotions enables you to learn to manage them. For example, anger-management practice may involve firstly increasing the sensation of anger through some of the techniques listed previously in a safe and comfortable environment, and then practising how to drop those anger sensations. Role plays use this concept successfully. The role players experience emotions directly, but through a filter of distance because they know they're 'playing a part'—making the emotions less confronting. A word of caution, however, is that before you start manipulating your very powerful negative emotions, you need to know you have the capability to bring them back under control. If you doubt you can, it's a good idea to enlist the assistance of a psychologist, who can help you learn to manage your emotions in a structured environment.

Research has uncovered the following about arousal:

- Everyone has a peak point of arousal at which his or her performance is at its best.

- A peak point of arousal is not the same for everyone, but it often sits roughly in the centre of the arousal continuum—somewhere between a comatose state and function at warp speed.

- A peak point of arousal varies depending on the nature of the task.

- How you interpret your arousal—as good or bad—affects your performance.

People don't spend long periods of time at their peak arousal level. In fact, they often slide up and down the arousal continuum throughout the day. In the mornings, arousal levels tend to be higher because people are energised about the day. However, by mid-afternoon—due to the human body's natural slowing of its Circadian rhythm—people's arousal levels begin to fall.

In high-arousal periods, your body experiences the following:

- Adrenalin is rapidly released into your blood.

- Your range of vision narrows (resulting in an exceptional but exclusionary focus).

- Your heart rate increases.

- Your blood pressure increases.

- Blood is sent to your major muscle groups in anticipation of the fight or flight reflex.

- Your immune, reproductive and digestive systems slow down.

- Your count of blood thickener increases in anticipation of physical trauma.

- Your normal information-processing methods are bypassed in favour of less accurate, but faster information-processing systems.

By contrast, during low-arousal periods, you experience the following:

- Your range of vision becomes very broad.

- Your heart rate lowers.

- Your blood pressure falls.

- Blood flow becomes less concentrated in your major muscle groups.

- Your immune, reproductive and digestive systems function normally.

- Normal information-processing methods are used for your intake and synthesis of information.

- You develop a higher level of distractibility.

- You begin possessing lower levels of motivation and energy with which to execute tasks.

- You feel sluggish or tired.

Arousal levels hark back to prehistoric times and the fight or flight reflex. In other words, when faced by a sabre-toothed tiger in the

Ice Age, you would have had to very quickly decide whether to run from it (thereby increasing your heart rate and the flow of blood to large leg and arm muscle groups) or fight it (leading to your blood thickening in anticipation of trauma). You also would have had to react at a nanosecond's notice—and your survival would have been dependent upon the length of that reaction time (faster but less accurate information processing systems).

Learning and creativity

When you want to acquire new information or a new skill, you require lower levels of arousal. This is because at a physiological level, you need a broad range of vision to absorb the information you see and its context; at an information-processing level, you need to be thorough in the analysis and application of the new information being fed to you; and on a self-belief level, you require the confidence to say to yourself that it's okay to make mistakes when you're learning. If you don't possess that mindset, you won't be capable of properly giving the task a go.

However, it's also pretty vital that you are not at the point of dozing off to sleep when you're in learning mode. Athletes, for example, can frequently find it tough to sufficiently manipulate their arousal levels for training purposes because they usually derive most reward from playing or competing, so training can be a necessary evil. Training is about skills acquisition—and athletes need sufficient focus and drive to learn and encode that information. But if they have low arousal levels, athletes can become easily distracted and therefore miss out on acquiring the necessary skills. Smart coaches know when their athletes have low arousal levels and will address the issue at the start of the session—usually with an emphasis on goal refocus and bursts of high-octane physical activity.

There are parallels in areas other than sport too. Think back to the last workshop, seminar or lecture you attended in which your eyelids felt heavy and the outside world seemed more of a distraction than usual. How much information do you think you absorbed during those times of high fatigue?

Creativity is also likely to be stifled by very high or very low arousal levels. Creativity requires a high degree of brain productivity. It entails the generation and analysis of ideas, and an assessment of their interconnectivity and best fit for your target outcome.

Translating this to other performance locations, consider your own workplace situation. You may need to hold a number of roles that require different skills. For example, when leading a meeting, you need to have the capacity to synthesise a number of different pieces of data; possess your target outcome for the meeting, thereby ensuring that discussions are pertinent to that outcome; be aware of individual communication styles so that you can act accordingly; and ensure overall clarity for a plan to move forward. Given the number of issues your brain has to deal with, it's vital that your arousal levels suit the task. If your arousal levels are too high, your faculties will be significantly affected, and if they're too low, your distractibility will increase — placing you at a disadvantage.

There are a couple of things you can do to boost your arousal levels to a point at which they're more effective. One is to conduct a short, sharp bout of exercise. Stepping is usually the most effective type of exercise because it will raise your heart rate faster than a short stroll will. However, if there are no steps or stairs in your vicinity, it can also help to stride in a purposeful manner at a moderate to fast pace for at least a minute or two.

The second exercise for boosting arousal levels involves 'adrenalin memory'. Memories can have an incredible influence on your thoughts and behaviour. You can choose to harness some of that power and use it to your advantage. Recall what would be a high-adrenalin moment for you. It could be a roller-coaster or horse ride — any situation that includes a little of the 'fear factor' but exuberance at the same time. Once you've identified your particular memory:

1   make sure you're in an area where you won't be interrupted

2   close your eyes

3   take yourself back to that moment. Where were you? Who was around you? What could you see, touch, smell, hear and taste?

4   feel the release of adrenalin into your bloodstream as you relive that adrenalin-pumping moment

5   open your eyes.

For the next couple of moments, you'll have enough adrenalin flowing to initiate some positive actions — whether it be a spot of exercise to help perpetuate the arousal or the ability to walk straight into a meeting feeling really pumped. Bear in mind, however, that the adrenalin will only last for a couple of minutes before it no longer has the same effect, so ensure that you give yourself an adrenalin memory 'injection' just before you need the boost.

Decision making

Effective decision making is about the acquisition, evaluation, synthesis and intended application of information. As such, arousal levels need to be sufficiently high for you to feel engaged by incoming data, but low enough for you to process that data effectively. Mark McBain, a former head coach for the Queensland Reds and a past Queensland player, believes his position as hooker and captain was not always compatible from a decision-making perspective. He says he needed to be at a high arousal level for the degree of contact with the opposition that playing in the front row required, but that when he had to make decisions, he was forced to consciously bring himself down from that level in order to think clearly.

When their time is short and their arousal levels too high, people tend to make decisions based on an instinct that is derived from past experience and the rapid application of that past experience to a similar situation. In a dynamic game like rugby—in which fast decision making is usually the order of the day—good players are often labelled as 'instinct players' or as having good 'game sense' because their decision making under pressure tends to be accurate.

On the other hand, instinctive decisions are far from comprehensive in terms of their assessment of all incoming material. When time is more readily available, it often pays to 'drop arousal' so you can make more considered and rational decisions.

Although you still need the capacity to rapidly decide on a course of action, sometimes a more comprehensive approach is better. You also need to ensure that your arousal levels are appropriate for your role—if your bubbling levels of frustration are threatening to erupt, then the chances are your decision making will be solely instinctive and therefore a great deal riskier.

Training versus competition

Different roles require different levels of arousal. The mental preparation undertaken by rugby players before a big game illustrates this phenomenon perfectly. Although personality has an impact on how players prepare themselves before playing, the physical requirement of the position that each player holds also has a significant influence. For instance, those players in the front row—in which a high level of physicality and contact is required—tend to really pump themselves and their arousal levels up to reach a point of controlled aggression that will lend them additional 'oomph' for scrums and force the play forward.

However, the players on the wing and at the back tend to take a far more relaxed approach to pregame preparation. They often have a bit of chat and chuckle among themselves and sometimes try to distract themselves from the upcoming game. Those players need lower levels of arousal because their roles on the field require a broad line of vision, and an ability to synthesise information from a number of areas and make effective decisions. If players in these types of positions are too pumped, they run the risk of 'choking' and failing because they won't have the mental capacity to fulfil their function properly.

Consider the topic of matching arousal levels to roles outside the sporting domain. For situations that you believe require you to 'perform'—such as giving a speech or presentation—perhaps a higher level of arousal is likely to be more effective for you in those performances. People employed in roles with significant responsibilities—in areas such as sales or group facilitation—may find that they require higher daily levels of arousal for peak performance. However, for those employed in tasks that require analysis or creativity, lower levels of arousal are likely to lead to more effective performances.

Needless to say, there are also moments when different arousal levels are required. The classic example of mismatched arousal levels within a management setting is the traditional manager who sets great store in the philosophy, 'They who yell loudest get the best outcomes from their people'. In this example the manager is only working at a high arousal level and is disregarding what the role may require at different times—such as enquiry, counsel or evaluation, which come with low arousal levels. To facilitate peak performance, you need to acquire the ability to match your arousal level to your situation. There are times when you will need to raise those arousal levels, and there are times when you will need to drop them. Consider your role—are you matching your arousal level to the requirements of your situation?

Making adjustments

Remember that it's the way you interpret your emotions that has the biggest influence on your behaviour. Because emotions combine to produce your arousal levels, it's the way you interpret your emotions — such as anxiety — that affects your arousal levels and therefore your performance.

So if you think to yourself, 'Yikes! I'm way over-cooked on this! The last time I was this nervous, I completely blew out!' then the chance of you performing well is poor. However, if your interpretation of that high anxiety — and therefore — high arousal is, 'Wow! I'm feeling so pumped! Nothing's going to touch me!' then success will be much more likely for you. Therefore, you need to possess a good awareness of your emotional reaction to your arousal levels preperformance — and then adjust them as necessary.

Some arousal is actually a good thing — it means you're more 'on the ball' and faster with your reactions. If your arousal levels are encroaching on your performance, here are some tips from inside the sporting arena that you can adapt and apply in your life to turn that around:

- *Breathing.* It sounds basic, but focusing on taking deep, rhythmic, cleansing breaths — without holding your breath at any point — acts as both a distraction from your high-arousal thoughts and a physiological relaxant. Be aware of the regularity and depth of each breath — suck in the air and feel it being absorbed, and then exhale the 'black smoke' of negativity from your body. Do this at least five times.

- *Live-ualisation.* Live-ualisation can also be used to increase or decrease your arousal.

- *Progressive muscular relaxation (PMR).* This is a very useful technique that can be applied in a variety of forms, depending on the amount of time available. The full version is recommended for those who have difficulty shutting down their brain and body when they go to bed. Because sleep is such a significant influence on performance, PMR can have an immediate impact. It is based on the principle that physically feeling the contrast between taut and relaxed muscles in your body relaxes you. First, you develop your awareness of taut muscle groups in each part of your body. Then you consciously relax each of those muscle groups systematically—fully experiencing the sensation of decreasing muscle tension. Starting with the top of your body and then working your way down through each muscle group is an effective strategy. Appendix C contains one of my favourite approaches to effective PMR.

▫ *A particular aroma.* I strongly believe people's olfactory organs are the forgotten ingredient in enhanced performance. Real estate agents, for example, assert that properties with wafting scents of freshly ground coffee and baked bread tempt potential buyers. Many people also advocate the relaxing powers of aromatherapy. But what about the scents that are uniquely evocative for each person? You may, for instance, walk into a room and catch a waft that immediately takes you back to a specific point or person in time—initiating nostalgia and the emotions connected to that memory. Similarly, to help themselves relax and sleep before major away-game competition, some athletes pack a pillowcase that smells of home. Alternatively, by always being in relaxing situations with an aroma of their choosing, they can develop a link between relaxing experiences and particular scent. They then add that scent—lavender, for example—to a tissue, which they will then sniff at times of performance anxiety to curb their anxiety. You too can harness the extraordinary and immediate power of smell to evoke emotion. It may involve using an association that is already there (such as the scent of your partner's perfume or aftershave) or building one of your own by always linking certain activities to the scent you want to associate them with.

▢ *Music.* Those who have already discovered the influencing power that music can have over emotions will not be surprised by this suggestion. Depending on genre, music can uplift, inspire, anger, relax, sadden or gladden you, or propel you back to another time in your life. Many athletes, for example, use music as a precompetition preparation device; they compile their preferred tunes and listen to them as part of their routine. They also often categorise their songs under the emotions they evoke — such as 'psych up', 'chill', 'focus' and 'good times' — and then make compilations accordingly. To effectively use this in your everyday life, ensure that your compilations are updated when required or their power becomes stale. It's about using what already triggers your emotions, but in an organised fashion; it enables you to take control over which emotions you feel — rather than finding yourself at the mercy of negativity storms.

▢ *Recovery.* Ensuring that you have good recovery routines that effectively deflate the stress balloons in your body and mind enables you to meet challenges with approximately zero stress. If your recovery one night is insufficient, you will walk into your work environment the next day with a significantly higher starting level of stress. You only have a limited coping capacity, so you will possess considerably fewer resources with which to manage challenges — and therefore heighten arousal — if you haven't fully recovered beforehand. The vicious kick is that stress usually compounds upon itself by continuing to destructively influence performance outcomes — in other words, when people are desperate to perform well, too much stress will hamper their ability to do that and they will therefore stress further. An effective mental and physical recovery routine is the key to being able to competently 'back up' — to go from one high-stress day to another and still perform.

▫ *From mountains to molehills.* By breaking down the big picture into bite-sized pieces you will gain perspective on the challenges you face. Drew Mitchell gives the following excellent example of how this applies in his sporting life:

> Rather than think in terms of 'Hell, I'm up against the All Blacks!' I make myself break down the team into the individual players and study them closely for their habits and weaknesses. You then go into the game thinking, 'I know that bloke and what he's likely to do, so I now reckon that I've got a good chance to nail him'. It works wonders for building confidence.

Drew's strategy works wonders for controlling arousal levels—and a genuinely confident, focused athlete is likely to be in almost perfect alignment with his or her arousal levels. So if formal meetings give you a case of the screaming heebie-jeebies, ensure you know your material and then break it down into component parts so that you can understand how each part operates. Alternatively, you could also divide the meetings up into time segments—for example, try obtaining meeting agendas ahead of time and focus on each of their sections. By doing the preparation ahead of time, you'll enter with increased confidence and decreased arousal because you'll be feeling much more in control.

Ability — knowledge and skills

Do you know what you know and what you need to know?

Miranda Banks

When it comes to achieving high performance in a team, Eddie Jones is considered and confident in his view:

> First, you need to get selection right. You have to identify people who can play better than they are at present. It's then about

putting together the squad—[by thinking about] skills, and physical and personal characteristics—in a cohesive way. Then you have to be able to coach the team. You need knowledge of the game and you have to be able to teach that knowledge in a transferable way. Lastly, you have to be able to manage the group. You need to know the players and understand what you have to do to get the best out of individuals as well as the group. The same goes for your staff. You have to know them and what you have to do to get the best out of them.

Eddie's story clearly demonstrates that you need a clear picture of the skills and knowledge required to achieve your particular target. This assessment phase, or 'exploration platform', is vital. It requires taking the time to thoroughly research the exact nature of your target and what is required to achieve it before executing your approach. Removing the pressure of having to make a decision straight away about the best path to take can be a huge relief for many people who feel confused about 'which road to take'—it validates their feelings of wanting to find out more before committing to a pathway. On the other hand, holding back on launching into action can be immensely difficult if you tend to be an 'action' person rather than a 'planning' person. However, taking the time to thoroughly assess all possible pathways and their manner of execution is likely to save you resources in the long term. In other words, just as exploration drilling is conducted before installing a more permanent and effective pipeline, so too will your own exploration reveal a better and more parsimonious approach to your performance.

Making a particularly relevant remark about the role of knowledge and skills in sport, Australian Wallaby Paul McLean says, 'You need a reasonable understanding of what you can and can't do. It's hard to solve a problem if you don't know there is one'.

Once you comprehensively understand the possible pathways, skills and abilities that will potentially take you to your target, you need to conduct a 'knowledge and skills audit' to assess whether you possess what's required for you to succeed. If you discover that you don't, ask yourself if you're going to acquire those skills somehow or outsource them. Again, there are a number of approaches that can be taken.

George Gregan and his wife, Erica, run a number of coffee shops in Sydney. Although an acclaimed champion on the rugby paddock, George is quick to admit that his skills as a barista were, at best, limited when he started out. He says, 'Erica coached me on how to make coffee. She's the brains behind it all and manages the day-to-day running of the business. I had to learn from her.'

George's experience illustrates the concepts of acquisition and outsourcing—he acquired the skills of a barista through Erica, but outsourced to her the management of day-to-day operations.

Acquiring and outsourcing the skills and knowledge necessary to achieve targets can also be used effectively for team performance. Terry Oliver, for example, uses discussions with other sporting coaches to develop ideas and concepts that—with some tweaking—could apply to his state cricket team.

Take a similar approach to your development. First identify the skills and knowledge that you wish to acquire and then identify the individuals or organisations to which you can outsource the abilities you don't have. In other words, become the general manager of all that information; organise and synchronise it so that it can be implemented in a way that will help you achieve your target. For example, you may wish to set up a consulting business. After spending time on your exploration platform, you deduce that there are a couple of areas of knowledge and skills that are likely to be important to your overall success. As a result of your skills and knowledge audit, you decide that you want to acquire a few additional skills of your own in specialist consulting. However, you also believe your company would be better served by outsourcing your information technology needs—rather than by you learning about how to design and manage websites. Your responsibility is to coordinate the inclusion of those outsourced skills in a way that meets your overall target.

Many people desire to change their career direction or overcome career 'speed humps'. It's particularly common in professional athletes who realise that they need to one day make the transition from playing sport to working in another occupation. Often, these individuals set up their own exploration platform — perhaps by contacting tertiary institutions for advice on courses and scheduling in study. In fact, they generally investigate most study-related options. However, they usually don't meet with anyone performing in or employed for the role they're interested in. But it's helpful for them to discover the direct and indirect networks of people that are related to that role and then aim to speak to between three and five of those people.

It's important to note that these conversations are not of a job-seeking nature, but are instead about gathering information from people who either employ people in that role or who fill it themselves. These conversations often produce some unanticipated results. Indeed, one senior manager reported that when he sought information about a role at a different organisation, his contact person said, 'I didn't realise that you were looking! That's great news!' As a consequence, he was referred directly into a position that was a great fit for him.

Another client of mine was unsure about how to improve the morale of her team. She thought her only real option was to 'bring in some experts' because her experience in the area was limited. But rather than outsource, she ended up finding a useful mentor in her own extended network who had experienced some similar issues in the past and implemented some successful strategies to cope. With some modification, those same strategies were implemented by my client, and she saw an immediate change in her team as a result.

I have a friend who — having been involved in heavy machinery operation for six years — wanted to make the transition into construction management. His less-than-mediocre approach to study meant that the university pathway was likely to be a long and challenging one. However, after conversing with a couple of key contacts in the industry, he discovered that he could start off as a trainee with a construction management company. That way, he could experience the nature of the work, earn a few dollars and possibly even have the company pay for his ongoing tertiary study. He followed through on it and the approach worked for him. In fact, he was promoted within the first month due to his work ethic and previous experience in heavy machinery.

Exploration and assessment time is vital. Not only does it grant you the opportunity to determine the knowledge and skills required to reach your goal, but it also enables you to investigate how you could potentially go about gaining them. The process may involve a mentor, study, advisers, taking on other roles or perhaps even recruiting experts to assist you.

Acquiring decision-making skills

A skill you may wish to develop for yourself is the art of effective decision making. It's one of my top-ten favourite skills to acquire. Decision making is a complex process, but it can be broken down into some simple rules:

- People tend to make decisions based on the outcome of their previous experiences. Specifically, a decision resulting in a good outcome will make people more likely to repeat that decision, but a bad outcome will make them more likely to change their decision.

- If people make decisions in an area frequently enough, the decisions will become automatic—or 'default'—and less effort intensive.

- When in high-pressure situations, people tend to make decisions based on their gut instinct or intuition.

▫ How comfortable people are with making decisions based on gut depends on their experience with the material they're working with and their personality type. Some personalities are more analytical and so prefer more conscious, measured decisions — whereas other personality types are more impulsive and prefer intuitive decision making.

▫ Confidence in decision making is only likely to increase if people practise making decisions. So if they spend their time in highly structured environments that don't require them to make decisions, it is unlikely that they'll feel confident about making decisions when it's needed.

This last point is particularly relevant. If you want to acquire or outsource decision-making skills, then you and the person you're outsourcing to must find opportunities to practise making decisions.

This is particularly evident in the rugby union. Rugby is a highly dynamic game. There are a number of 'set pieces' and items of structure within the game that are predetermined, but a large part of the game also relies upon players making decisions during play. These decisions are made under huge pressure — just imagine a 100-kilogram member of the opposition hurtling towards you while you have the ball in hand! Decisions need to be made quickly and confidently, and they must be consistent with the game plan and its requirements. However, the outcome of these decisions is not always positive, and one of the key reasons for this is that players are not given sufficient opportunity to exercise their decision-making skills away from the game. Training is structured and repetitive — making it appropriate for the acquisition of certain techniques but completely inadequate for developing and enhancing decision-making abilities. Players, in the professional era, have the option of occupying themselves away from the rugby paddock and some choose not to, thereby further minimising their opportunities to develop those cerebral skills. Timetables and schedules are structured and the players directed to minute degrees to maximise efficiency. Yet despite a dearth of training in the discipline, these players are expected to suddenly produce accurate, speedy and confident decision-making skills during high-pressure game situations. To be effective decision makers, coaches need to address the common neglect of this area.

To improve your decision making in time-poor situations, it helps to adopt a structure that can be applied to the decision-making process. The following steps give an example of a structure that could be applied to the process and used effectively:

1   Ask yourself, 'What am I aiming for?'

2   Ask yourself, 'What do I have here. What are my options?'

3   Decide and execute that decision.

Then practise the technique over and over again for common decisions that you make daily. Although it will feel a bit peculiar at first, after some concentrated practice, it will become your default approach to decision making—and it will happen so fast that it will seem to be synonymous with your gut instinct.

Example 4.1: making decisions under pressure

Now apply this to the life or death situation included in the introduction. Your aim is obvious—survival of you and the others under your care within the cave. What you have is a potentially large threat—or is it?

In the blink of an eye, you need to determine whether Moggins is a threat or not. If you determine that the threat is real, you will run through the options—give up survival; fight with the nearby spear, attempt to escape with the others through the busted escape route, try to recall how to reason with lions, hide and hope the lion goes away or pass the challenge on to someone else. You decide that your best chance of survival is to grab your spear and — with a stirring war cry — launch into the fight. In a second you decide and execute. Fortunately for you, the lion decides that its potential meal is too annoying so early in the morning, so it departs.

You've just gone through the first three steps in your decision-making structure. The more practice you give yourself prior to facing decisions, the faster you'll become at processing each step. It's why people train — and the more closely your training matches 'game day' execution, the better. You just need to consider the situations that may require intuitive decision making and then train for them. The military has been doing it for years and so have many of this country's athletes. What about you?

Another way to hone your decision making is to — as mentioned earlier — practise the process for similar situations over and over again. In sport, video footage of games can be very handy for doing this. The coach plays the tape of the game for a short period, stops the tape, asks the player, what should happen next — giving minimal time for an answer — and then continues to play the tape to compare the player's answer with actuality.

This process enables sports people to learn to objectively anticipate what should happen next in the context of real-life action. The more they practise deciding on outcomes within a split-second, the greater their confidence in decision making during similar play will be. It's about training what coaches refer to as 'game sense'. Some players are naturally gifted in this regard, but others benefit from the opportunity to improve it.

You can apply the same process to your life, using the 'video recorder' of your mind and doing the following:

1   Identify common situations in which you have to make split-second decisions.

2   Practise playing through scenarios in your mind.

3   Introduce different elements to the scenarios each time.

4   Pressure yourself by imposing a time limit within which to make a decision about what to do next.

Involving family and friends to play out roles can also help. You can use role-playing to fabricate the pressure of real-life scenarios. The more frequently you practise, the more confidently you'll start making those decisions. When your confidence grows, your speed and determination when executing decisions also increases.

Some situations that require split-second decisions lend themselves to manipulation and you'll find that you can actually slow them down to provide you with more thinking time. The key is to recognise when those situations arise; some of them may feel urgent, but closer analysis may indicate otherwise. For example, my advice to coaches with whom I work is that if they feel ambushed by a parent or athlete suddenly demanding sensitive or controversial information (such as selection issues), is to firmly tell them that they recognise the importance of their problem and that they'd like to make a time to talk through it. The coach can then schedule a time and each party can prepare some points to address at the meeting.

Coaches can feel the pressure to act urgently when a parent or athlete raises a sensitive issue with them. This sense of urgency stems more from the coach's arousal levels than the needs of the situation though. In any case, it's not a good idea to address emotive issues and it's generally not vital that the answer be provided immediately. Instead, the response should be postponed to minimise the emotion related to the potentially flammable incident. Those involved will then still feel sufficiently acknowledged to settle down until later circumstances are more conducive to an outcome.

So can you think of examples in your own life in which situations might have appeared to be urgent, but could easily have been played down and managed more calmly by rescheduling to another time?

If you're wishing to improve your decision-making skills in the workplace, you need to be given ample opportunity to practise when the outcome isn't so vital. Ask for increased chances to decide on opinions, courses of action and recommendations. Use meetings and discussions as a forum — and even if your input isn't requested, mentally work through the path that you would take in the situation under discussion and make a decision. It's similar to betting on a race without putting down money — there's a process of selection, but no pressure in regard to the outcome. Remember also that imposing structure to all aspects of work is marvellously efficient, but it tends to stifle dynamic decision making. Maximise your development by including decision-making opportunities regularly.

By this point, you should have a clear and comprehensive understanding of the knowledge and skills required to achieve your target and be able to identify whether you possess them. If you don't have the ability necessary to achieve your target, you need to decide whether to acquire or outsource. If you do choose to outsource, you need to know how you should go about locating that resource. Remember to add those necessary points to your to do list.

Ponder points

> Are you managing your emotions? Are you maximising your immersion in positive emotions that drive you forward?

> Are you in control of the destructive emotions that lead in the opposite direction to goal achievement?

Ponder points (cont'd)

» What skills and knowledge do you need to achieve your goals? Spend time on your exploration platform and fully research that question.

» Do you currently have what you need? Conduct a self-audit to find this out.

» Are you going to develop the skills you require yourself or are you going to recruit experts?

» How do you go about making decisions?

» How do you tend to respond in situations of urgency?

» Do you think that you would benefit from using a structured approach to making decisions?

» Have you identified decision-making situations in which the outcomes are likely to benefit from practice?

Chapter 5
External drivers

Having looked at the internal forces that drive you and their impact on your behaviour, now turn your attention to your external drivers. Analyse each external driver of your behaviour from the perspective of achieving your BOMOAG. This chapter aims to deepen your understanding of each driver, the effect the drivers have on you and what strategies you can implement to align your behaviour to your goals.

Your external drivers of behaviour are the people around you, the places in which you spend time and the things at your disposal.

People

At the start of each new season, a team's management will sit down and look at how to improve the team's performance from the year before. From head coach to team dietitian, all of the team's advisers will reflect on the year past and plan for the year coming. The athletes themselves will set their goals for skills development, strength and conditioning, and mental enhancement. By working with each member of team management, athletes incorporate updated sections into their individualised plans for development.

Team and squad athletes have an advantage because their support network for development is already set up around them. By being recruited into a group, they have been given support before they even start playing. Athletes in individual-based sports, on the other hand, usually have to recruit their own support networks. For example, a seriously competitive triathlete will need to recruit a number of coaches for swimming, cycling and running, as well as for fitness, nutrition and mental-skills training.

That generally applies to most non-athletes too—people need to recruit their own support networks in order to access the information and encouragement required to develop their own plans for achieving their targets.

Filling in the gaps

No-one is designed to be good at everything, so it helps to surround yourself with others who can assist you. Terry Oliver expresses it well:

> I don't lead with a lot of structure nor do I personally need it but I need to have others around me to supply that structure to fill the void. I have great relationships with my immediate staff and I also have the support of my superiors along with the capacity to be honest. We trust each other on face value.

Rod Macqueen, one of Australia's most successful rugby coaches, takes a similar approach. He recognises that his role was not to be everything to everybody, so he recruited a team around him and adopted the role of team leader.

You probably tend to visit the same doctor, dentist, hairdresser or bank manager for expert advice, but what about your group of friends? Does that network also enable you to 'fill in the gaps'—from information on footy games to opera to life's challenges? Do those networks of people celebrate achievements? In other words, are there key people in your 'team' who can assist you in areas that are not your strongpoint?

You'll gain tremendous value from learning from others. After all, each person who contributed knowledge to these pages is a testament to that. Even if you just pick up a single tip that carries you that little bit faster towards your target, imagine how handy a record of all of these valuable snippets of advice would be.

If you were to make a list of all the pieces of advice given to you over your lifetime, it would probably begin with the heading, 'Things my mother or father taught me'. However, the list would become longer as more people come into your life and your pool of advice deepens. I mentioned in the section on recovery a useful technique called a 'sunshine book'—in which you record positive comments you've heard, the positive emotions you've felt and the positive situations that have happened to you, so that you can refer to it when you're feeling less than sunny.

There's also a lot of value to be gained from making a similar book entitled, *Things I've Learned So Far*. At the end of each day, write down a note or two in the book about what you learned that day. You can then use it as a review tool down the track—using it in a similar way to how this book should be interpreted (as a whole heap of tips for 'life training'). It would also be a useful tool to hand down to your kids.

Energy pumps and energy parasites

Friends give us wings when we forget how to fly.

Anonymous

'Energy pumps' are the people in your life who radiate energy; 'energy parasites' are those people who suck your energy dry.

It pays to sit down and identify where the pumps and parasites exist in your interaction network. Janine Shepherd hits the nail on the head when she says:

> Good relationships are one of my must-haves. I believe that we're all connected on an energy level. I know that I need to be around positive, energy-giving people, otherwise I walk away feeling completely drained.

Sometimes you can't help but be around a parasite—it may be a manager or colleague with whom you have to work, for example. However, you can plan to manage the occasions when you have to be around those types of people—and then 'refill' your energy levels as soon as you can.

On the other hand, you also have energy pumps around you; they are those awesomely brilliant people who radiate warmth and energy as easily as they breath. My brother, Donald, for instance, is one of my greatest energy pumps. Donald is one of these magnetic people who pulls everyone to him—he enters a room and people are drawn to him like bees to a honey pot. He has a rare ability to make everyone who talks to him feel that he or she is worthwhile—and he may only be my little brother, but there's nothing little about the effect his energy has on me! Barb Barkley echoes those sentiments:

> It's so important to be around positive people. When I returned to Sydney from the US, I broke myself down and then rebuilt myself. There have been times when I didn't believe in myself. I'd return to my family—they knew who I wanted to be when I didn't know myself. Believe in the universe, but consciously choose to be around positive people.

Being around the right people can also enable you to retain your perspective on what it is you do and the value of your effort. It's vital to identify your key energy pumps. They may be family members, friends, work colleagues or team mates. In fact, they don't even have to be human; pets, for example, can be immensely valuable—as can places such as gardens, parks or beaches.

Equally, choose not to be around energy parasites as much as you can. Sometimes you can 'trail' parasites—people you've known for years through one connection or another who have simply just always been around. However, by auditing the energy pumps and parasites in your life, it will remind you that you have a choice when it comes to spending time around certain people. So if you don't need to spend time with them, don't do it.

People can often be energy parasites at times and energy pumps at other times. This is frequently the case with people closest to you—whether family members or close friends. You are probably so open to them that you're also open to whatever energy they're sending in your direction. So you need to improve your ability to rapidly identify whether someone is a pump or parasite at any given moment—and then choose whether or not to stick around. Of course, there are occasions that call for you to be an energy pump to others in their hour of need. You can derive considerable satisfaction from that warm, toasty feeling that comes from helping others out when they need it. But you should develop the ability to make a choice about the types of people you want in your life. If you make that choice consciously, you will have a far greater capacity to monitor and manage your energy output, and will be as efficient as possible in how you send out your energy to others. Your energy is limited; you need to manage it as effectively as possible.

If you find yourself being the energy pump for everyone else most of the time and never seem to receive any energy back, you need to give yourself a speedy lesson in locating and accepting energy from others. Don't feel wildly guilty or weak for seeking something from others, because to function effectively, you need to be in a state of balance—energy in and energy out. If you're poor at asking for energy back, then you'll hit the bottom of the tank pretty quickly. To balance your energy, look for the little things that may help—such as spoiling yourself with a massage, asking someone else in your household to cook and clean up dinner one night or sitting quietly with a book and having 'me time' rather than running around doing things for others. In other words, start small and build from there. Remember that achieving your energy balance is the key to maintaining your vitality and confidence.

Role modelling

Prominent athletes are often referred to as role models. They typically possess the ability to influence others either consciously or unconsciously, just by being. A role model himself, Eddie Jones has the following to say about the responsibilities of being a role model:

> I'm lucky to be in the position where I can touch a lot of people. I'm conscious of being a role model and I regard it as very important. You have to live the culture that you want the team to have, but you also have to set realistic expectations. I once heard the owner of Saracens Rugby Club say, 'Never try to be perfect. Just try to be reasonable'. That made sense to me. We're not perfect and we're never going to be. We just have to be reasonable and accept that being a role model is part of the job.

Having this capability to influence others brings with it responsibility—as Eddie says—and also reinforces the fact that a single person is able to change another person's behaviour.

Role models within teams can also have a significant influence on their team mates. For example, the 2005 season was a particularly tough one for the Queensland Reds. Results were poor and there was a feeling throughout the team—from the coach to the youngest player—that everyone had let the team down. However, after some soul searching at the end of the Super 12 period, the team witnessed some dramatic changes. Players from the team who were selected to play for the Australian Wallabies were absent—and several weren't going to be around for the next few months. Some players—David Croft and Sean Hardman in particular—put their hands up to assume the responsibility of leading change.

Whether evident at training (at which you could hear positive feedback and support given to players) or at team meetings (at which certain players led discussion and then facilitated communication between the players, coaching staff and even the board), some players had the determination and talent necessary to be outstanding role models. The younger, less experienced players looked to them for direction—and it was given to them firmly and effectively. When the Wallaby players returned, they—Chris Latham and John Roe in particular—lent weight to that team support. Their efforts paid off. The team established a cohesion not witnessed for some years—and it was due to that original base of support that they could begin to rebuild winning performances.

Accounts in the media often highlight the occasions when sports role models fail to uphold the responsibility that comes with that standing in the community. However, you don't need to be a high-profile athlete to possess role-model responsibilities—once you start achieving in your area of expertise you too will be able to wield influence for good or evil. Equally, people are not only driven to use high-profile individuals as role models; they also often unconsciously select someone they admire from inside their circle of acquaintances.

Phil Hogan makes the comment that people should be careful about whom they choose to be their heroes. So if you choose to look up to a role model, select the person with caution. Although someone may have achieved the success to which you aspire, his or her pathway to that outcome may be contrary to your belief and value system. Remember though that you can choose the behaviours you want to model; you don't have to emulate all of your role model's behaviours. For example, you may be unimpressed with the disorganised way someone you admire maintains his or her affairs, but that same person may be an excellent role model due to his or her ability to lead a meeting or discussion and effectively construct an argument. Sifting through the skills and abilities of a number of potential role models can often produce some exceptionally useful results—without you feeling the need to model your entire existence solely on one person.

Mentoring

Mentoring, like role modelling, is a term often used in the literature on performance coaching. A mentor is someone who has already successfully done what it is you're aiming to do. A parent—or perhaps a teacher or an extended family member—is likely to be someone's first ever mentor. A mentor has already experienced the pitfalls along the journey and is happy to give advice about dealing with them. Mentoring differs from role modelling in that—although a mentor may indeed be a role model—a mentoring relationship is far more active in nature. Role modelling is passive to the extent that the role model may not even be aware of his or her influence on others, whereas a mentor is aware that he or she is an integral and active part of someone else's development.

Having a mentor is advantageous because it enables you to liaise, communicate and be supported by someone with significant experience in the area you operate in; mentoring also has the benefit of providing someone you can defer to who has a personality or communication style that you can effectively work with.

However, mentors should only be used for a specific part of your life—such as your career, education or child rearing; a single mentor will not mentor everything in your life. Having said that, many people have cemented long-term, successful connections with mentors who they turn to for a helpful perspective, regardless of the topic.

Successful sportspeople are usually very happy to talk about their mentors. Australian Wallaby Drew Mitchell has the following to say about his mentors:

> Dell [Wendell Sailor] and Lath [Chris Latham] were my greatest influences both at Reds and Wallabies. The thing that's pretty

amazing is that we're in direct competition for spots on the side as we pretty much play in the same positions, but they still really help me out. Both of them used to tell me when I first got into Wallabies and was really nervous that I was there because I'd earned it. When we're on the paddock, they always give me positive feedback when I do things well.

As a player, Chris Latham's among the toughest critics of his own performance; he expects high standards to be set and met. However, if you were to watch a training session or game of his, you'd hear him peppering his talk with specific and targeted positive feedback to players around him—and they would clearly respond to it.

Like role modelling, mentoring also comes with responsibility, and it's essential that the mentor is comfortable with that. As Dr Sam Goldstein discusses in his work on developing mental resilience, you need to identify your mentor and also act as a mentor to others. That way, you can balance your learning intake with your teaching output—enabling you to understand how to be effective because you'll have experienced what it's like to be on both sides of the relationship.

I've set up a number of mentoring programs with sporting teams, schools and individuals, so I know matching mentors to subjects is not always easy. Personalities—as well as experience and expectations—need to be matched, or to at least sit comfortably with one another. Matching experience and expectations should be the easiest part, yet too often is the expectation component—about who does what and when—glossed over. Even if the personalities between two people match ('Yeah, she's a really great person and we chatted for ages'), if expectations aren't set from the start, the mentoring process can break down rapidly in today's time-poor environments. So work out with your mentor from the outset both of your expectations for the mentoring process, even if it is done informally. How often will it happen? Where will it happen? What outcomes should be achieved? The commitment to mentoring can then be made in full understanding of what lies ahead for both of you.

When attempting to identify a suitable mentor for yourself, it is vital that you ask yourself the following questions:

❑ Is this person sufficiently experienced in the area to assist me with my process of learning and discovery?

❑ Does this person have a communication style that I can effectively operate with? (Your mentor does not necessarily need to be your buddy, but you do need to have open and clear communication.)

❑ Does this person have enough time—as well as the inclination—to act as a mentor to me? (The approximate framework for communication—how often and by what means—should be established early in the relationship.)

❑ Do my expectations of being mentored by this person match his or her expectations of me?

Once you answer these questions affirmatively, you'll be ready to develop an approximate schedule for contact—including meetings, discussions and reviews. It should also tell you where and when you're meeting, and if there will be any follow-up meetings. If you and your mentor have set your expectations beforehand, this process will be fairly straightforward, and the degree of mutual commitment will be clear.

Form your own team

In rugby, groups of players are frequently referred to as 'playing units'. They're the players who share very similar process goals for performance—and the tighter the unit, the greater its power. For example, before their respective retirements, Nick Stiles and Fletcher Dyson—both members of the Wallaby alumni and former experienced Reds players—formed a particularly tight unit. They derived obvious support from each other in terms of the positions they played as well as their friendship away from sport.

Think about someone you could form a unit with. It is generally not a mentor, but a peer—someone who understands your situation but who also brings value to the table. Nick and Fletcher, for instance, have very different personalities, but they seemed to draw strength from those very differences because each could provide the other with an alternative perspective to a challenging situation.

Those in your 'team' may not always be there to tell you how brilliant you are or how perceptive your decisions have been. But in a true and trusting relationship, negative and positive feedback must be given—as Barb Barkley says:

> I have to seek intense honesty. When I emerge from a pressure situation, I want to be around someone who knows me implicitly and with whom I can talk through the negatives. They're a sounding board, but they're also incredibly honest. I can then return to the scene of the pressure situation and think far more clearly.

Phil Hogan also has a point to make about the role of feedback in teams:

> My wife Michelle is a solicitor who graduated with honours in Law—she's a very smart woman. We work together as a team. As we've set the goals together, we both know and have agreed upon what we want to achieve as a family. We each have busy days, but after the kids have gone to bed, we sit and talk and compare notes. It keeps us on track and gives both of us the strength of a team approach.

Like Phil has done with his family, if you can recruit all your family members into your team, the chance of you reaching your goals will be magnified.

A sense of belonging

Related to the idea of forming your own team is the concept of feeling a sense of belonging in a group—as demonstrated by Abraham Maslow's hierarchy of social needs. Elton Flatley describes a couple of examples of this in his life:

> One of my best games was in 2002 at Twickenham. Wallabies versus England. I'd played a test or two, but wasn't a regular in the side. This time though, in my mind, running on, I felt that I belonged, rather than having the thought of no mistakes. This time, I'd go out and enjoy myself—which is what I did. And I played one of my best games.

> Belonging is really important to me. I remember the 'two for tuesdays' dinners with the boys when I was only eighteen. We used to go around to Jason Little's house for dinner. It made me felt like I belonged—that I had to work hard, but that I was accepted. I now try to do the same with the young players coming through. I spend time with them, teach them a few pointers and form a good relationship so that they feel comfortable coming to see me on and off the field.

People need to feel they belong somewhere. A sense of belonging comes from being in a group whose values and corresponding behaviours you identify with—and who identify with you. If you feel a sense of isolation in a group, it can often be because your values are in conflict with group thinking and behaviour or others are unaware that they have similar values to you. If your values and corresponding behaviours are the same as those held by others in the team, then it's merely a case of taking the opportunity to share them with one or more group members. But if your values and behaviours differ from those of other team members, the chances are that you'll always struggle to find a sense of belonging—and would be much better off looking for it elsewhere.

Your values and how you prioritise them can also change over time, so it's not surprising that sometimes you may find yourself on the outside of a group to which you once belonged—not because of any one event, but simply because you 'drifted apart' from it. Starting work, getting married or having children are all the types of significant events that can trigger a change in priority in your values and behaviours. They are the times that you usually need to review the groups you belong to and consciously decide whether to continue your commitment to the group, become a 'part-time' member of it and accept the consequences or leave the group and locate one more suitable for you. Don't feel guilty about your decision. Life is a journey that includes you encountering different people at different points along that path. The key is to recognise those people for the impact they will have on you before you begin to feel torn.

The most vital point to bear in mind though is that you need to feel a sense of authentic belonging to at least one group. If you no longer gain that from your old group—despite the voice of denial speaking in your head—then you need to find another. More importantly, really make the effort to find it. Identify your newly arranged priorities and values and match them with those of other groups of individuals in your workplace or social community. Invest time in those matches and allow your sense of belonging to grow.

If you keep a skill to yourself, it doesn't multiply. By sharing talents and abilities, you then promote the growth and consolidation of your team. As Archie Douglas says, 'If there's one word I'd select for ensuring success within a team it's "sharing"'. You also facilitate a great sense of trust—thereby ensuring that when you really need your team to perform, you can call on the most effective group of people to help you because they will have learned to share their talents and their loads with you.

On a related point, when you have established your group, or 'team', to gain the greatest benefit for everyone, it really is a simple matter of putting in so that you can take out. (After all, if a farmer never plants seeds, the harvester can never take ears of wheat.)

In other words, when you see opportunities to assist or develop others in your team, never shy away from offering to help. If you do that it will serve you and your team well in the future — as long as you have selected your team mates well.

Networking

The person whom you think won't do anything for you will probably be the one who'll do the most.

Phil Hogan

Okay, so you've developed a strong, immediately available team for yourself, but what about broadening your horizons by networking? You've probably heard the line, 'It's not what you know, but who you know'; well, there's a lot of truth in that statement.

However, it's important to network with the right people. There is, undeniably, positive power around positive people — and that energy transfers itself with a fabulously compounding effect. Just as Gestalt philosophy proposes that 'the whole is greater than the sum of its parts', so too does having a team of positive people around you multiply that power. Vicki Wilson gives a good example of this:

> In 1994, Marg Angove, the Australian netball coach, brought in some bush firemen to speak to the girls during preseason. Those guys had a fire go right over the top of them, but they stayed together in the truck, so they survived. Those guys told us that if you want to confront firestorms, then you're better off doing it by sticking together.

The story illustrates that each firefighter was a whole lot scared, but also a little bit brave. So if you were to just add up the emotions in that truck, you'd end up with a large heap of fear and a small heap of courage. But by sticking together, the power of the group's cohesion meant that bravery was multiplied to the point that it overcame the fear.

Unsurprisingly, group power can produce the same effect with destructive emotions—making it even more essential that the people in your group harness that power for good. Phil Hogan also has a great story about the benefits of networking with the right people. He reveals:

> The night before we opened our new bar, Jade Buddha, Dave Rafter [promotions manager] and Gary [Phil's brother] were testing new cocktails in a bar. A guy came into the room and stood beside them. I was there too and remembered him from years ago in one of our earlier clubs. Chris was just a young bloke on the floor of the club with a couple of mates.
>
> Anyway, I went up to greet him and he introduced me to his friends. One of his friends was called Max, and Max told me that he was the son of Chris's kung fu teacher—and he offered us a dragon. What you have to understand is that this new bar of ours has an 'East meets West' theme, but we'd decided against having a dragon because of the organisation [it required]. Here's this guy who's wandered in and offered to get a dragon from one of the places at which he worked and would organise it for free. That dragon was a massive hit at the opening. Pat Rafter remembered the dragon. Everyone remembered that dragon. I just figure that you create your own luck and karma will do the rest. We needed a dragon and a dragon walked through our door because we'd remembered a young bloke from a long time ago.

Phil's story demonstrates the power of a simple act of courtesy. By making a point remembering someone's name—and by taking the time to welcome him personally—he encouraged good luck to head in his direction.

George Gregan's tip on networking is also simple: 'You meet lots of people, but for it to be useful, you need to know where you're going'. In other words, if you have a clear picture in your mind of your target outcome, you'll be far more likely to attract the right people. You'll also increase the chance of something positive happening, because those people will also be clear on your desired outcome. Whether that outcome is as simple as increasing your network of contacts in a specific area or developing a better way of hunting out some good advice on investments, keep that clarity in your mind. Vicki Wilson believes having a target of meeting people also has its benefits:

> Be brave enough to leave your comfort zone. I was invited to attend the launch—the official opening of the Yatala Brewery. I'd responded that I'd attend back in January, but when the day came, I really didn't feel in the mood. I had board papers to read and there were a hundred other things to be done. But I'd said yes, so I went.

> I was one of three women in a crowd of two hundred. I set myself the target to meet ten new people—to make a conscious effort to move away from always standing with people I know and introduce myself to others. You don't need to hang around for long—just have a chat and then move on. I came out of it feeling great!

Vicki's advice demonstrates that setting yourself a target before going into an unfamiliar social environment is a smart move. It gives you focus and a challenge and can therefore be rewarding. Also, making yourself a mini list of conversation topics and possible questions ahead of a social gathering will enable you to feel armed with the right tools from the start. If your conversation starts to falter, you can refer to the list for some inspiration.

Talking tactics

When you have a clear handle on the chat that you use to others, you will have far greater control over—and influence on—the eventual outcomes of your interactions. It is about increasing your self-awareness.

'When I have to say something honestly that's not particularly positive, I'll be honest, but I'll also do it in a way that doesn't devalue a person', comments Barb Barkley. She goes on to say:

When I worked with Wayne Bennett at the Brisbane Broncos, I picked up a lot from him. He treated people in a way that gave them his expectation of them so that they would always do the best they could. That expectation then became a self-fulfilling prophesy—and I'd actually see them make behavioural changes to encourage that prophesy.

Tony Wilson reflects similarly:

I take the philosophy that no conversation you ever have with anyone is neutral. You can either inspire people or you can drag them down. You have to understand that everyone has their own 'reality'. The things you say that you may think are straightforward or even irrelevant may not be for them—just because their perception of reality is different from yours.

Barb Barkley's advice, 'People may not remember what you say, but they will remember how you made them feel', underscores the importance of consciously choosing and being aware of the characteristics that you project particularly when using your networking skills. 'Choose who you want to be', she says. 'When you enter a room, be conscious, responsible and respectful when you impart yourself onto others'. Vicki Wilson adds to Barb's comments by saying, 'Build your aura—come across as a happy, confident person and that's what people will remember. That's what I want people to remember'.

When asked about her strategic approach, Vicki Wilson points out that you may also want to consider the practicalities of that initial meeting:

I've changed my drinking hand. I now drink with my left hand, so I can shake hands with my right! ... I'm also initially reserved with people. I like to hold back and not show my full hand until I work out on the map where they fit and how they operate. Sitting back and observing is immensely valuable—especially if you know that you're going to need to work with them.

On developing conversations, Barb has some further advice:

Find some common ground and develop that topic. I refer to it as filling in the nooks and crannies. All of a sudden, you're on your way to developing a relationship characterised by openness and expression of genuine interest in the other. That's what having a human conversation is all about. It's also the most effective.

A part of making a good first impression is considering your declarations and promises and remaining cautious. 'My advice for working with people is to under promise and over-deliver', says Ben Tune. 'It's the same for networking. I'd never make a promise to someone I'd just met unless I knew beyond a doubt that I could carry out that promise. And I'd make sure I did'.

So if you say you're going to do something for someone, write it in your diary or notebook then and there. It will let the other person know that you were serious about your offer—and it will act as a memory cue for you. Then ensure that you follow through on your promise so that your initial good impression is consolidated by your behaviour.

The art of reciprocity

Do unto others and they will owe unto you.

Tony Wilson

People often find it difficult to say no when asked to do something in the workplace. However, if execution of a task is within your control, emphasise to the person asking you that the action is out of the ordinary for you; it will minimise the chance of the person expecting that behaviour to be repeated as part of the normal course of events. Tony Wilson describes here how he implements this practice in his workplace:

In business, I take the approach to let those others know when I'm doing them a favour—that it's above and beyond the call of duty. If you don't let them know and simply acquiesce to every demand, for starters they'll end up undervaluing you and your product and, over time, they'll take those 'additional things' for granted. Essentially, it'll eventually leave you both out of pocket and looking like an unreasonable person if, all of a sudden, you start complaining about it.

Also, business is about give and take. So if you grant a favour, you have the right to ask for one in return—as per the usual social and business etiquette. It's a good idea to ask for that return favour, however, before your execution of the original favour is forgotten. For example, often, when a sports team changes its management, the athletes who did a favour for the team in expectation that it would be returned when they wished, find that the passing of time and new management has erased memory of the original favour.

Places and things

Now this may sound like a peculiar point to make, but your geographical position can have a significant impact on the ease and speed at which you motor towards your targets.

The facilities available at your geographical location can play a huge role in a decision to move. There may, for example, be a university that offers a better course or a company office that provides better experience elsewhere. Also, athletes who live in country areas often have to decide if and when they need to move to a larger urban centre to access a higher standard of training and competition. Unfortunately, athletes making that sacrifice can find that losing that home environment results in the loss of one of their key sources of strength and wellbeing.

For others, making the move away from large urban centres to rural areas can be the balm that's required to achieve life balance and the speedier fulfilment of targets—so even if it involves a little extra travel, the benefits are seen as worthwhile. Simply put, you need to consider your personal targets and ask yourself whether you're in the best possible place to meet them.

Where is the place that you make decisions? Knowing this is also a worthwhile consideration. To give an example, Queensland Rugby did not have their administrative headquarters at their playing ground at Ballymore for many years—even though it was where all the players and coaching staff were based. As a consequence, administrative staff and management found it far more challenging to build and maintain relationships with players and coaches because they had to make a concerted effort to 'be around' them. But when the team's headquarters were moved to Ballymore, the integration of staff and players led to more successful outcomes.

You may not be located in the best position to conduct your work at your workplace. For example, I have a good friend who works in administration for a state government. She struggled when she was moved between departments because her desk was relocated to a spot some distance from the senior manager she was meant to be supporting. So communication between them became challenging and often broke down. However, after discussions with her manager, her desk was moved to a position more conducive to open communication between her and her manager.

Reflect on your geography in relation to all that's important to you. Increase your awareness of the potential influence that locations may have over your situation and plan for or make adjustments that are within your capacity to change.

Coaches and athletes alike talk about the importance of having the right facilities to do a job. Terry Oliver, George Gregan, Elton Flatley and Bennett King believe that if you don't have the right equipment, it makes it near impossible to get the job done—let alone to get it done with an optimal result. Take a look at your own facilities and maximise their effectiveness by looking at what you can control. Good facilities cost money; excellent facilities cost even more. This fact is known well by Eddie Jones, who says:

> I had the opportunity of visiting Arsenal's training centre in the UK. It's the best I've ever seen and I could just smell the influence of Arsenal's manager all over it. It was simple, white, unostentatious and completely geared to performance. It would have cost a huge amount. I know we're all restricted by money, but we don't always realise how much of an enormous effect that can have [on output].

Your aim should be to balance your needs and resources—and the projected benefits of investing in improved facilities. Ask yourself what you need, then prioritise that list and begin the acquisition process.

It's not a matter of attempting to acquire everything—a prioritised list will help you decide what facilities are necessary.

So rather than risk wasting money, think beforehand of the facilities that would be the best fit for you. Make a list of what you require to function effectively in your workplace and write down the impact that meeting those needs will have on you—and then prioritise them. Let the people who possess some control over those facilities know and start to make the changes that you can.

Your environment plays a significant role in your ability to be effective. Janine Shepherd, for example, says that having a good home environment is very important to her. She says, 'I set up my house environment—clean all of the spaces and now it has a great feel and loads of positive energy'.

Your home needs to engender refreshment, recovery, comfort and security. When you next walk into your home, consciously look around and be aware of what feelings it evokes. Janine mentioned that having clean and clear spaces is effective for her. What works for you? It's a philosophy that can be applied to all areas in your life—including work.

Work needs to encourage focus but also carry your own individualised 'stamp', because it is the area where you spend much of your time. Ask yourself: Do I have things around me that will remind me to be effective? Are my work targets easily visible? Do I have something in place that enables me to take recovery breaks when required?

Ideally, it is best to allocate different areas to different parts of your life—and then try not to overlap. For example, work should occur primarily in a 'work space', and recovery in a 'recovery space'. That way, the visual cues associated with being in a certain place will trigger your brain to automatically think along certain lines. This is particularly true for anyone who has undertaken study. If your study and play areas overlap and you attempt to study, you'll be far more likely to become distracted by the more attractive 'play' cues—and it will therefore take much longer to encourage your brain to develop a state of mind that is conducive to study.

Ponder points

- ⇒ Who are you spending your time around?

- ⇒ Who are the energy pumps and energy parasites around you? Do you have plans in place for managing the results of spending time around energy parasites?

- ⇒ Do you have role models and are they effective?

- ⇒ Do you use a mentor and is he or she effective?

- ⇒ Who is on your team? Do you have the right people to help you along your path?

> ➤ Are you always on the lookout for effective people to add to your team — even if it's for the outer rather than the inner circle?
>
> ➤ What are your environments like? Are they assisting you to achieve your goals or do they hamper your efforts? Can you improve them?
>
> ➤ Make a list of the things that you need to execute your activities well. Prioritise them and start to make changes that are within your control.
>
> ➤ What's your people environment? Who's your support network?
>
> ➤ What are the gaps that need to be filled?

Chapter 6

Behaviour alignment

It may sound strange initially, but there is a bedrock of truth in the statement, 'Behaviour leads to behaviour'. You may describe the experience behind it as 'being on a roll' or as 'finishing what you've already started'. Both remarks highlight the fact that engaging in certain behaviours increases the likelihood of other behaviours following.

When coaches talk about being on a roll, they often say that it can lead to either success or disaster—achievement or failure; for example, a hockey coach relates his experience of this with one of his youngest players:

> He's a pretty good kid, gets on well with the others in the team, and really enjoys his hockey. The only thing is that he's not so good when things change around him. Take, for example, a couple of weeks ago. He usually likes to arrive a bit early,

organised and ready to go for the game. He puts his bag down and then goes about his normal routine—including a bit of a chat to the others, making him generally calm and relaxed, which is how he likes to play. He's a key player for the team and also a good leader because he does tend to have that calm about him.

The problem was, two weeks ago he was running late to the game—it was something to do with having to collect his sister. I knew things weren't great as he was pretty flustered—rushing around and not really talking to anyone. Since he was running late, I also noticed that he wasn't in his usual position in the dressing room—someone else had taken his spot. I went up and had a quick word to him, but he didn't really listen to me.

That game he didn't play well and actually ended up giving one of the other players a mouthful, which he'd never done before.

As that example shows, you need to examine your behaviour in the same way. Which of your behaviours results in something constructive and what do you do that leads you into trouble? If you start the day by declaring, 'Today I'm feeling good', you will increase the possibility of you indeed feeling good and therefore performing well.

But what about your other behaviours? Consider your destructive behaviours—such as pressing the snooze button on your alarm clock, skipping breakfast or being caught up in gossip sessions—that lead you into further destructive behaviour.

You also need to be able to identify behaviours that will enable you to re-align yourself to your pathway—so that you can get back on the 'good roll' when things have started going awry. Take a look at the behaviours that you need to demonstrate in order to achieve your BOMOAG.

Making sacrifices for your BOMOAG

Always bear in mind that your own resolution to succeed is more important than any one thing.

Abraham Lincoln

Resources, especially time, are usually limited, so you will frequently have to make sacrifices in order to reach your BOMOAG. By having a clear picture of why you're making those sacrifices, your determination to change will increase—a view echoed by Rob Metcalfe, who advises:

> Having a clear [BOMOAG] helps you to decide what it is you don't want to do as well as what it is you do want to do. It's then easy to answer the question, is my current behaviour helping me to achieve my overall goal?

Top athletes around the world recognise the need for sacrifice. For example, Toutai Kefu, a former Australian rugby player, only drank Diet Coke throughout a sports awards night dinner because he had 'Wallabies training first thing in the morning'. Likewise, one of the youngest Wallabies players left his good friend's eighteenth birthday party early in order to be in good shape for physical testing the following day.

Jenny Hyde, a representative for Great Britain in the equestrian event of showjumping, has the following to say about the sacrifices she's made for her sport:

> Sometimes my friends get pretty angry with me because I usually don't have huge nights out and stay over. I often have a competition on the weekend and I just feel that I'd be letting down my horse, support team and self if I failed to turn up at that competition absolutely on my game. I don't not have a social life, but I'm a lot more choosy about the things that I do because my first priority is the dream that I have for my horse

and me. Maybe I wouldn't feel the same if he wasn't such a great horse, but he has amazing potential and I've been given this opportunity to make that potential come alive.

'If doing A makes you successful, then why do B?' asks Tony Wilson, Performance Coordinator for Queensland Cricket and Australian Baseball. He talks about how important it is to evaluate whether your behaviour is providing you with the best results:

Know what works and do it consistently. Do the little things well. Don't suddenly change what have previously been effective techniques solely because you're not going well right now. It's a mistake that so many people make. If those techniques have been consistently successful in the past, then chances are it's something else entirely that's making you perform badly right now.

Vicki Wilson, an Olympic ambassador and the former captain of the Australia netball team, says that she became 'smarter' in her behaviour in the later part of her career:

In 1995 I did my knee and required a complete knee reconstruction. It was pretty late in my career, and Peter Myers, my surgeon, posed me the question, 'How much longer do you want to play?' I sat back and realised that I wanted to go to the next world championships, another four years away. Aside from continuing to enjoy playing, I also didn't want to have the last memory of my career as being carried off the court in excruciating pain.

Four years is a long time, so I realised that I had to become smarter in my playing and training. I paid every attention to detail—no cutting corners. I spent a lot of time talking to the trainer and physio about the best recovery program for me—and really understanding what it was that I needed to do. Then I rewarded myself. I'd train hard during the week—wanting to prove that [even though] I was over thirty, I could still play with the best. I would then take time out on the weekend and go up the coast or go scuba diving or whatever. I'd reward myself for my hard work. I'd learned the importance of having balance and proper recovery that was both mental and physical.

Of course, the final reward was that after those four years, I made it to the next world championships.

Vicki gives very sound advice — if you're working hard to achieve your BOMOAG, remember to reward yourself for that hard work, especially if you follow a long-term program. The last thing you want to do is burn out before achieving peak performance.

So being clear on your BOMOAG will help you to be more efficient at evaluating whether your behaviour is conducive to reaching it. If your current behaviour isn't helping you to achieve your overall vision, why engage in it? Also, if certain behaviours have been consistently helping you to achieve your goals in the past, the chances are that they will be useful to you again. Consider your experiences of past successes, re-implement the behaviour that coincided with them and stick with those behaviours. Finally, work smarter — by increasing your knowledge about what needs to be done before embarking on your plan — and then reward yourself for your hard work.

Processes — not outcomes

Once you've set your BOMOAG and milestones, balanced your life wheel by ensuring all life areas are being managed and dedicated your mind to your BOMOAG commitment, you need to be specific about the behaviours required to achieve what you want. Then the operative question becomes about how to do that. BOMOAGs are the point on the horizon that you're aiming for, but if you were only ever looking to the horizon and never at the job at hand, you'd never get there. What behaviours are you going to focus on?

It's essential that you focus on processes instead of outcomes. A process is all about the how of a journey, rather than the what at the end of it. Golfers constantly have outcomes in their mind due to the leader board being on display. It spells out in black and white—and in large letters—who is winning. But winning is a tricky outcome because it's not within your control—due to it being partly dependent on the competence of your opposition. The key is to focus on the processes that will help you achieve your ultimate goal. For example, golfers may choose to focus on managing their arousal levels via breathing control or on making small corrections to their technique. Both are processes that can lead to successful outcomes.

By focusing on processes rather than outcomes you are essentially doing two things—distracting yourself from the anxiety and pressure that comes from a focus on winning, and refocusing on the how of achieving success rather than on what that success could be.

For example, when Susie O'Neill, a former Australian Olympic swimmer, was about to swim a record-breaking race, she was asked by a journalist if she was thinking of breaking Mary T Meagher's record time. Susie replied that she did not think about it at all because she was solely focused on swimming her own race. In other words, Susie focused her energy on the process of swimming—something that was within her control. This enabled her to achieve the success of a record-breaking swim.

Set daily goals

I recently taught counselling skills at a residential school for Victoria University. A completely unexpected pleasure was the participation in the class by Olympic champion Cathy Freeman. In one of the sessions, we discussed the importance of setting process goals as frequently as possible. I mentioned that some research had been done with Olympic athletes that attempted to identify what sets Olympic medal-winning athletes apart from other Olympians. The study found that those who won medals set goals for each training session—not just for competition. Cathy, in her inimitable way, looked aghast and said, 'Of course you set goals for each training session! That's just a part of being a successful elite athlete!' The idea of not doing so simply hadn't entered her mind.

Cathy's comments demonstrate that the more frequently you set goals and timeframes within which to achieve them, the more successful you're likely to be—as long as they're process goals and their achievement is completely within your control.

For most people, those goals manifest themselves in the form of to do lists. It's an effective approach. Develop a routine in which you list and prioritise your goals at the start of each day. However, there are traps. Make sure that there is a realistic number of things on the list for the time limits you've set, that you don't become distracted from key priorities and that you are assertive about sticking to your agenda when others want you to help them with theirs.

Avoiding the traps

To avoid many of the traps associated with unrealistic to do lists, after you've written your to do list for the day, prioritise each item on it and then roughly assign an appropriate period of time within which to complete each task. If you end up with a list for the day that adds up to eighty-six hours, you will know that you're starting out on the wrong foot. Equally, if you're happy with your calculations and launch into the day only to discover that you've seriously underestimated the amount of time required for certain items, take a moment or two to review and restructure. After all, daily targets are about meeting goals in order to feel a sense of achievement— they're not about feeling a sense of incompetence due to non-achievement.

At university, distractions tend to arrive in the form of half-dressed bodies running in waving drinks vouchers for happy hour at the local bowling club. Although what constitutes distractions in your life will change over time, they usually maintain their destructive power. So you need to be effective at assessing the nature of your potential distraction, and the matrix in figure 6.1 should help you to do that.

Figure 6.1: the distraction-assessment matrix

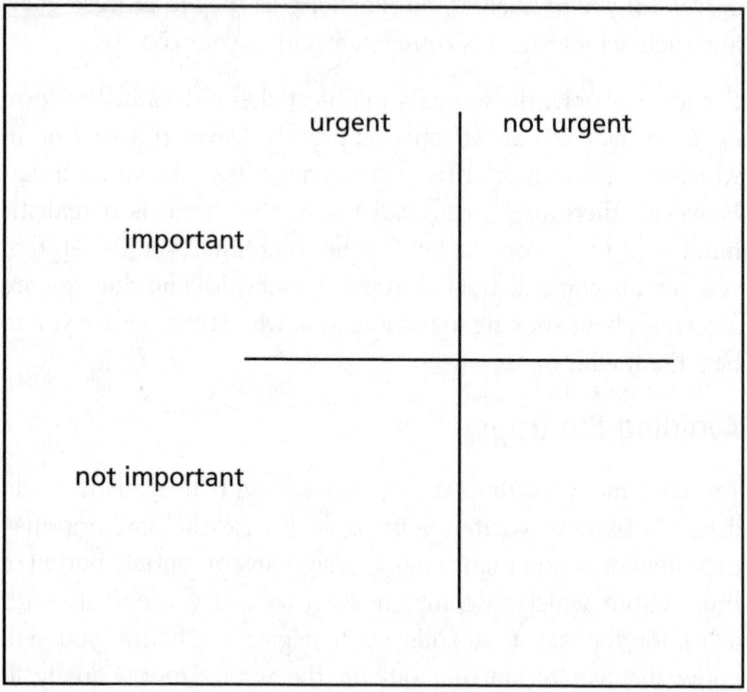

Once you've worked out the category that it sits in, you'll be in a better position to deal with it. You'll know whether it is better to:

□ deal with it immediately (urgent and important)

□ reschedule it to a more convenient time (important but not urgent)

◻ resolve it shortly (important but not urgent — although it may become urgent if left for too long)

◻ ignore it completely (not important and not urgent).

There are many people who need variety in their day and find distractions almost a welcome change; they need to work smarter to keep their focus. Most elite-level coaches only run training sessions in short blocks for that very reason. One coach, for instance, makes the following relevant remarks about distractions during training:

> It's amazing how grown men will become completely distracted by a plane flying overhead. A plane! Half of the group will look skywards as though they've never seen a plane before!

So if you know you're the type of person that would be distracted by a plane overhead, then conduct short, concentrated bursts of work and allocate discrete windows of time for alternative activities. After a while, it will become habitual.

Assertiveness

Another trap to avoid is saying yes when you really want to say no. Assertive communication is about being in the middle of a continuum in which aggressive communication (including angry, violent or generally offensive communication) sits at one end and passive communication (constantly giving in and saying yes to people until you reach a point where you want to wallop someone) sits at the other end.

Being assertive requires being politely firm when asking questions, giving your opinion or declining requests. It's win–win communication because the message is clearly delivered and the person receiving the message doesn't feel as if the rage of a thousand maddened camels is being directed at them.

Assertive communication is a habit. So if you're used to taking a passive approach in your life outside of work, there's a strong chance you'll do the same in your work environment. The secret to mastering assertive communication is that you need to start small—and with situations that aren't wildly important to you. For example, you may want to practise by asking to have something added to the next meal you order out—such as sauce on the side or extra mustard. Get into the habit of giving specific feedback to wait staff—point out the great things about the meal and then point out what could have been improved. You may never eat in that restaurant again, but at least it gives you practice in giving your opinion when there's less pressure involved. Of course, don't just pick out hospitality workers—try doing it while shopping. When you're in a store and receiving help from the shop assistant before buying something, give the person some feedback. In your opinion, what did you like about the experience and what could have been improved?

After a while, you'll feel comfortable about giving your opinion and saying how you feel in social situations. The next step is to progress to being assertive about little things in your work environment—such as by making a note of some specific points you would like to bring up at the next meeting. Consider how you could value-add to your team or project. If necessary, rehearse what you want to say at the meeting beforehand. Then, when you're at the meeting, take a deep breath and have your views heard.

By practising giving your opinion, you'll feel more comfortable when others come to you with issues that you need to postpone to another time. An easy tactic is to tell them that you 'understand the matter is important' and you 'therefore need to allocate the proper time towards it'—and then look in your diary for an appropriate time. If it is outside your area of expertise or interest—and the best answer is not to postpone but to decline—an alternative approach is necessary; for example:

> I can appreciate that this is important to you, but right now I have higher priorities that need to be completed beforehand,

and I'm unsure when I'll be finished. I'm sorry, but this time I'm not able to help out.

If you're dealing with someone who is used to you giving in to his or her requests, he or she is likely to behave in a similar way to the child in a supermarket who is used to being given treats on demand (on initial refusal, the child becomes louder before becoming quieter). However, you need to stand your ground until that period passes or—after giving the person a specific directive—leave the room because you 'need to attend an urgent engagement'. After a while, he or she will learn what constitutes acceptable behaviour around you.

Assertiveness is all about being in control of the expectations others have of you. If they expect you to acquiesce to every request, you'll have made a rod for your own back because they'll expect you to always say yes. To start to remould those destructive expectations, take time to tell people about your priorities for the day—by saying, for example, 'These are the things I'm going to focus upon today. If it's outside of those areas, then it'll need to wait'. By doing that, people won't be surprised when you turn their requests down.

Good and bad habits

Tradition is a guide, not a jailer.

Somerset Maugham

Some industries love and embrace change because they are constantly focused on the 'next big thing' but have little regard for what has gone on in the past. There are also industries—like some sport-related industries—that will hang on to traditions like a dog to a bone. Neither situation is ideal.

Just as regular reviews of your behaviours and targets is beneficial, so too is it a good idea to review your traditional approaches and activities. You can learn from the past and examine what has worked, what hasn't worked and why. You can then look at the challenges currently facing you and selectively choose from your traditions in order for you to meet your targets. However, if you begin to feel too much pressure, you will default to your habits—regardless of whether they are the best fit for you. Those habits will then become more entrenched—making it more likely that you will select one of them in the future.

Once you've taken a look at your everyday habits and decided on their value, apply the same scrutiny to your habits under pressure. When the going gets tough, what do you tend to do? Pressure is alive and well in this fast-paced world, and people usually engage in daily practice to handle it. At work or home, certain situations will apply pressure to your limited coping capacity and increase your levels of arousal.

Having worked with a number of coaches and teams, I've witnessed some interesting responses to intense pressure. That pressure can manifest itself in a player as frustrated anger; yelling and cursing at other people; self-directed cursing only; complete withdrawal from a situation and everyone involved with it; quiet manipulation by people who see an opening to push their own agenda; floods of tears; or aimless roaming with a dazed expression.

On the other hand, coaches and teams can improve under that pressure and turn situations around. For example, Vicki Wilson accepted the post of head coach to the Firebirds, a state netball team. The team had failed to win a single game in its previous season. As a great of the game, Vicki was under intense pressure due to people's expectation that she produce wins. Her approach was to allocate responsibility—the players had to meet the high standards of training and competition set by the team; the leaders within the team had the role of setting positive conditions; and Vicki and her assistant coach, Kylie, shouldered responsibility for coaching and managing all external forces, thereby freeing the players to engage in what they did best. The Firebirds began looking good—in a preseason competition with New Zealand, the team won their first games for eighteen months. They then finished the season having made it into the finals for the first time—which was not bad for the 'wooden spooners' of yore.

The results were telling. By understanding how you react to pressure in any given situation, you'll be better able to anticipate and modify your response when necessary. Consider your moments of pressure and how you tend to respond. If you can see some room for improvement, try making the effort to improve things. The results will speak for themselves.

Digging in your toes

It doesn't matter how slow you go, as long as you don't stop.

Confucius

Successful author and Brisbane music icon Barry Bull says, 'No is negotiable'®. Barry has run Toombul Music for twenty-five years and now spends a fair portion of his time passing on his wisdom to others. His music store is well known for hosting a wide range of live music acts. Demonstrating his belief that 'persistence beats resistance', Barry relates one of his own experiences:

Sir Cliff Richard was releasing a new album. Now I'd developed a pretty good relationship with Sir Cliff, so I planned on putting a cocktail party for his fans for an early release of his album and I wanted to speak to Sir Cliff regarding an interview. I emailed Sir Cliff's secretary to suggest it. The response back from her was that it wasn't an option since Sir Cliff was in Barbados at that time. I replied that he'd do something for me. I was right; Sir Cliff agreed to do an interview with me on Brisbane's radio, 4BC, so we set a time up.

As luck would have it, we were unsuccessful the first time due to time change problems, so I emailed Sir Cliff's secretary again to reschedule. Eventually, we confirmed a time. I called the station and organised a studio and I had a great interview with Sir Cliff Richard.

The way I look at that episode is that if I'd given up when Sir Cliff's secretary first told me that Sir Cliff was unavailable, then I'd never have secured the interview—nor the subsequent successful album sales.

When talking to Barry, enthusiasm for forward motion emanates from him. His success as a retailer in a highly competitive industry is understandable when you consider that he refuses to accept that 'no' means 'never'.

Like Barry, rugby coach Eddie Jones also believes in standing your ground. Speaking about his toughest coaching gig yet, he says:

I'd just been appointed to the coaching position for Tokai University in Japan. It was my first professional coaching job. I was in charge of eighty students who played in first division, but who always came last.

My challenge was to increase performance—which meant changing the culture from a historically based preparation to a sports science-based preparation.

The first three months were the hardest, but there was no way I was going to give in. I suppose I don't have a fear of failure—I'm happy to give something my best and know that it will be worthwhile doing so.

Eddie's remarks reflect two things. The first is that once he's accepted a role, he doesn't give in but instead digs in his toes and shoulders the load. The second is that he has a strong belief in his coaching ability—he knew that if he gave something his best shot, it would be a worthwhile exercise with positive results.

To dig in your toes, you need to believe in your ability to positively affect events—despite the challenges in front of you. Without that belief, you'll be hard-pressed to maintain the momentum you need to continue along your path.

Perseverance

Faith is the bird that feels the light when the dawn is still dark.

Anonymous

Achieving your goals doesn't always happen overnight. Kellie Hogan, a sports dietitian, often has to work with athletes who want to increase muscle content and decrease fat. She describes this experience:

> It's human nature. People always want immediate results or they want it yesterday and athletes even more so. Muscle gain can be a slow process. Explaining to an athlete that gaining a kilogram of muscle a month is good going is always a challenge. It requires dedication and consistency and most importantly faith, in their training and nutrition programs and to achieve success. If they have this, it will eventually work.

Kellie encourages athletes to track their progress by diarising their skinfold measures and—when they feel their progress is stalling—to take a look back through that diary and reflect on the real progress that has been made.

AnneMarie White has filled many roles in her life—from PE teacher to sports journalist to speech writer; however, it is her persistence and determination that make her so inspirational. AnneMarie battled breast cancer and won, but she learned the value of perseverance long before being diagnosed. Here she describes how she learned that lesson:

> The inaugural position of CEO of the Sports Federation was being advertised. I applied, but I wasn't short-listed—seemingly because I wasn't male. I had to go to Perth to cover the nationals for water polo, but on my return, I discovered that I still wasn't short-listed. So I approached them and asked why and what it was they were looking for. I ended up having a long chat on the phone—which led to an interview, which led to the job that I held for the next three and a half years. It pays to be persistent!

Staying positive

Rugby player Ben Tune reveals something about his mindset when he says, 'If someone told me that by being depressed, you'd get better faster, then I'd do it. Since I don't think it does, I won't'. Ben would have to be one of the most pragmatic and mentally tough athletes around. He's endured numerous operations and committed to gruelling rehabilitation programs only to have injury impede his progress time and time again. His remarks about remaining positive in the face of considerable challenge are completely consistent with his approach to rugby and life.

Again, to stay on track you need to look at your BOMOAG and ask yourself whether indulging in negative thinking is going to help you. Instead, set daily targets that are within your realm of achievement and tell yourself, 'I can do it!' as often as you can. By not allowing yourself time to wallow, you're preventing yourself from engaging in a 'mental mope'.

If your inner sergeant, on the other hand, is failing in his or her duty to keep your mind disciplined, you may well find that you need to acquire some external assistance before the wallow becomes a deep, deep pit with impossibly steep and shiny sides. If being negative and depressed is a state of mind that you can't shake, hunt out some help in the form of a referral from your local doctor or make a time to see a qualified mental-heath professional.

Take responsibility

Discipline is a huge factor in achieving your goals—and it goes hand in hand with self-responsibility. No-one is going to be there pushing you 100 per cent of the time—that drive needs to come from inside you. Agreeing wholeheartedly, Barry Bull says:

> My theory is that progress is only made when you accept ownership for your destiny. I'm also driven by self-development.

If I felt I had no personal performance left to give, I'd retire, but for me, it's all about re-invention. I don't want to set boundaries on my life.

From a sports perspective, it's interesting to see the difference in attitude to performance between athletes in team-based sports and athletes in individual-based sports. Athletes in nonteam sports generally know from the outset of a competition that their performance rests entirely on their shoulders because if they take shortcuts, they know there will be no-one else to pick up the pieces and win the day. Athletes in team sports, however, often take far longer to accept full responsibility for their performance—because they know if they 'drop the ball', someone will run up and help them out of trouble. That mindset—demonstrated, for example, by a player saying, 'The game outcome doesn't rest on my shoulders alone, so I can afford to slacken off'—is reflected in training too. It can take a long time to eliminate that attitude in athletes—and even if their attitude does change, it will usually only happen when the athletes feel they're under the spotlight of individual attention—just as the individual athletes know themselves to be each day.

However, there are some outstanding team athletes who have taken their own personal approach to training. Essentially, the athletes set their own standards and regularly review their performance against them. Regardless of the views of others, their performance is monitored only against themselves.

How well do you accept responsibility for your behavioural outcomes? Do you push yourself harder when you know you've reached a plateau? Do you wait for someone else to do it for you—hoping that you'll be able to 'coast' until that time arrives? Remember that the only eyes you can't hide from are your own.

Regardless of your targets, the sooner you consciously take responsibility for your outcomes, the more efficient you will be at reaching your goals. You may have others around you to support your efforts, but they have their own hopes, dreams and worries to think about; in other words, you need to be responsible for your success.

Once you've made the decision—calmly and consciously—to do that, improving your self-discipline will come more easily. Remember that your choices ultimately affect your outcomes.

Recovery routines

Finish each day and be done with it. You have done what you could. Some blunders and absurdities no doubt crept in; forget them as soon as you can. Tomorrow is a new day; begin it well and serenely and with too high a spirit to be encumbered by your old nonsense.

Waldo Emerson

I used to have a little radio segment on Brisbane's 4BC *Nightshow* that the host, Tony Johnston, and I called 'Beating the buggeries of life'. It's about acknowledging that all the little things in life can accumulate and place pressure on your coping mechanisms. Having all the tools in the world won't make a scrap of difference if you don't know you have a crack in your foundations. It's vital to create a strong self-awareness of your thoughts, feelings and energy levels; if you don't, your coping mechanisms may collapse. But once you've located the weakness, you can match your tools to the situation.

Rob Metcalfe has some excellent reflections on increasing self-awareness:

> That period just before sleep—and then just after waking—are very important. In my presleep 'daze', I like to indulge in some fantasy regarding the coming day. Naturally, those fantasies are all related to storming success! However, for me, it's when I first wake up that I really ask myself what's going on.

First I ask myself what I feel good about: What's the day about to hold? What's good about how I feel? Then I ask myself, what do I feel bad about? I call it the 'hangover effect'. I ask myself, do I have a 'hangover' about someone or something that I need to manage before returning to work? I then have to compartmentalise—put it away in a box to deal with later. When the hangover is particularly bad, I draw strength from my goals and values; that is, I ask myself, was my past behaviour aligned to my goals and values? If so, then I'm allowed to forgive myself.

Without Rob developing a strategy for increasing his awareness of what's ticking over in his mind and its impact, his ability to manage those thoughts—and to anticipate their effect on his behaviour—would be limited.

Athletes clearly understand the importance of effective recovery. Without it, their ability to 'back up' with a valuable training session or competition is severely compromised. John Roe outlines the recovery routine he follows after a game:

It's not a particularly conscious process now as I've been doing it for so long. My big focus is on getting physical treatment from the physio and getting good sleep. After the game, I tend to go home rather than go out. I like to be in bed by 11.00 pm, which puts me five hours in front.

From a mental perspective, I take my time in the dressing-rooms and have a long shower, taking time to think back on the game. I'll be very specific about my reflections by asking myself: Was my mistake just prior to half-time because I made a decision to take the wrong option? Was I running the wrong line? Should my head have been under rather than over?

That way, I get to make specific corrections. I then shut myself off from that performance—though I admit that it takes longer to do so after a bad game.

Recovery time gives you the opportunity to work through your past performance in your head—analysing what went well, what went poorly and how you can improve. Finally, it provides you with some closure, or a resolution. After all, if you want to be effective, you can't spend your life peering into your rear-view mirror.

Changing your philosophy about work and life processes can significantly affect your overall output. It enables effective recovery time for you to rebuild you energy levels and re-open your mind. It can also indirectly improve the output of those who work for you—an important point for anyone in charge of running a team. Marty Duncan, for example, is a highly successful restaurateur. His restaurants—including Freestyle Emporium—are well known for their owner's warm and welcoming personal style; Marty's attitude seems to be appreciated by staff and customers alike. However, he is the first to admit that his ability to manage relationships hasn't always been straightforward:

> I have an extraordinary focus. I've lost two [romantic] partners because of the business. They just resented the time that I spent on my dream and livelihood. As far as I was concerned, my dream came first.
>
> When the first shop was five years old, I went on holiday for a month. It was the first holiday that was longer than four days that I'd taken since the shop had opened. It was so hard to leave my 'baby', but I knew that it was also good for me.
>
> I had a 'me day' in Byron Bay and realised that I was so buried in the business that the café wasn't Freestyle—it was Martin's Place. And I was expected to be there all the time by staff and customers alike. I realised that I had to change the way that I thought as it was sucking all of my soul, so I started to make others accountable by delegating. I gave my staff autonomy and also gave them ownership in the dream. Funnily enough, by creating a sense of belonging for my staff—where they were not just workers [but owners as well]—I created a better balanced life for me and for my business.

Ensure you find a strategy that refreshes you. Then systematically incorporate it into your days, months and years—while encouraging those around you to do the same.

The power of positive movement

When one moves positively in the direction of his dreams and attempts to live the life in which he has envisaged himself, he'll be met with a success unexpected in common hours.

Henry David Thoreau

Tony Wilson describes how he applies positive movement in his life:

> I usually get up in the morning and feel positive. If I'm not positive, I know I won't be successful, so if I'm a bit low, I'll use physical cues to get me mentally prepared for the day. For me, that usually means smiling and talking loudly and animatedly to people. If I don't and just sit down quietly in the dressing-rooms when I arrive there then I can pretty confidently say that I'll coach badly. I figure that if I keep moving, those inner demons can't get me!

Think about how positive movement could apply to you. (Ask yourself, what are the things I do that click my brain and body into action?) If you're a naturally highly interactive person, then alarm bells should start ringing if you're sitting alone and feeling morose. If that's the case, then make the effort to stand up and start chatting with someone you like—even if you don't entirely feel like doing so.

Laughter clubs

Laughter clubs are based on the principles of positive movement. A laughter club is a group of people who meet—usually somewhere outside—to laugh out loud. When they first turn up, many people don't feel like breaking into spontaneous laughter.

But they usually finish the session in genuine laughter because they've absorbed the natural energy-boosting effects generated simply by laughing.

Although laughter clubs aren't for everyone, you can apply their philosophy in other aspects of your life. For example, if you've made yourself focus on 'being happy and active in the morning', then stretch a smile when you rise from bed in the morning and walk briskly around the house—even when you don't feel like it. The rewards will set you on track to achieving your goals more effectively than wallowing in unmitigated grumpiness will.

The power of planning and practice

The single greatest predictor of positive performance is the perception of being prepared.

Miranda Banks

Planning is one of the key elements of preparation. So know what you're going to do, how you're going to do it and what you can control, and then develop a few safety nets for contingencies. For example, imagine that you are planning a presentation you have to give. You could plan that for the first five minutes, your focus will be on clearly presenting yourself and reading to your audience; for the next period of time, your focus will be on outlining the issues at hand; for the next block of time, you will propose the solutions; and in the final minute, you will reinforce your message. Once you've nailed your plan, you can then put it into practice.

Dietitian Kellie Hogan chuckles wryly when speaking about the preparation done by athletes on nutrition:

> We definitely get the full range. You can pretty much guarantee that it's the ones who've planned their meals, ensured their fluids are up and have sorted out their post-game recovery will also tend to perform better on field. Experienced athletes who have good self-awareness about their individual needs will make

sure that they're on top of their planning. I don't need to worry about them. My greatest concerns are those who never seem to get the message and who end up dehydrated or exhausted, so can't perform on game day or, worse still, on the training paddock, where the majority of skills acquisition occurs.

What I don't get is that it doesn't take much extra effort to plan and organise, yet there are still those who fail to do so and trip up. Eventually, they learn. Or they just don't make it any further and never realise their potential.

Practice is the other key element of preparation. Practice is essentially about rehearsing what you plan on executing. The value of practice is that you can repeatedly rehearse until you find it boring—and when something is boring, it won't prompt anxiety. The most important element of practice is to recognise the need to rehearse the reality as much as possible. For sports-competition preparation, for example, matching training sessions to game days is the most effective way to execute strong performance. So if you have an important interview coming up, practise being interviewed by someone you don't know—rather than your friend—because it will simulate the conditions of a real interview. Practice also involves discipline—a point emphasised by Vicki Wilson, who says:

> I had to get to the [netball] post six times a week, and two hundred shots would have to go in each time. It took a while to get the right routine and I'd get frustrated if it didn't happen.

Vicki's story demonstrates that she couldn't depend on anybody else to throw those shots—her successful performance was her responsibility, so she went the extra mile.

It wasn't simply her own performance that Vicki prepared for; she also compiled a book on every player she had ever come up against—rather than relying on the coach to give her the information. Reviewing that dossier gave her invaluable information prior to each game and she consequently had her own game plan and became very relaxed on the court. As the coach of the Queensland Firebirds, she now encourages each of her players to do the same—to take responsibility for their knowledge of the opposition.

When you're planning for your best performances, it pays to know what you're up against. Usually, the information is there if you look hard enough, but it does involve putting time aside to gather that information. Once again, it's about understanding that the key to good performance is the commitment of time to prepare well beforehand.

On that topic, John Roe says, 'One of my needs as a player is to be able to ask myself before a game, have I done what I need?—and then to be able to answer, yes'. The need for effective preparation is glaringly evident in John's remarks, but so is the importance of allocating sufficient time in your schedule for preparation. Archie Douglas makes a similar point:

> Know what you have to do and feel confident that you can do it. If you're fearful, then put the time aside to properly prepare. I'm not a confident public speaker—it's not something that naturally sits comfortably with me, so I take the time to make sure that I'm confident with what it is I'm delivering and to whom. I also take the time to practise. One of the great keys to success is being able to express yourself. So it's vital for me to take the time to make sure that I'm doing it properly.

In short, if you need to do something that would benefit your performance—but the mere thought of doing so turns your red cells white with fright—planning and practice is the key to relieving that anxiety.

Finally, it's important to attend to details and care of execution both in practice and actual performance. David Croft, a senior player for the Queensland Reds and a board member of QRU, communicates his thoughts on paying attention to detail:

> Now that we're nearing competition time, we really need to sharpen our focus on getting the little things right. If we

don't do it well now, then we're not likely to do it well come game time. It's a case of going out to training each day with a conscious focus on close attention to detail. It's exactly the same in business—if I don't get the detail right, then it reflects on everything I do.

Interestingly, that perspective is usually reserved for the top players; in contrast, mediocre performances reflect the viewpoint that 'near enough is good enough'.

So plan, and practise in conditions that are as close to reality as possible—making sure to consciously pay attention to detail when you execute your plan.

Being in the zone

One of the buzz words in sport is 'flow'. Conceptualised by psychologists Csikszentmihalyi and Jackson, flow basically describes your state of mind when you are feeling completely 'in tune' and relaxed while executing a task. A key characteristic of the experience is the feeling of being utterly absorbed in a task yet also at ease—making the task feel effortless. It is often accompanied by an overwhelming sense of positivity—as though things are going so well that you could continue doing the task forever. Dr Graeme Maw gives an example of how he sometimes coaches athletes into a state of flow:

> For me, it's more like role playing. For example, you may not be a great public speaker, but the key is to get into character—for that period of time, play the character who can speak in public well. It can work well for sport. Say you're a tennis coach. You ask one of your pupils to work on their forehand volley. They tell you that they're hopeless at forehand volleys and can't do it. You ask them how they'd like to volley, and they answer, 'Like Martina Navratilova'. So you answer, 'Show me how Martina volleys then'. It can have a really profound effect on athletes.

Playing a character to enhance your performance isn't only limited to sport. I've worked in the past with elite ballet dancers.

One particular dancer wanted to bring down her levels of anxiety. One of her upcoming performances required her to dance as though she was a trapped butterfly in a jar. To overcome her feelings of anxiety, she focused her mind on 'becoming' the butterfly. By completely absorbing herself in the role, she had no 'head space' left for anxiety. The exercise worked a treat.

For those who would like to develop self-confidence and a strong sense of self, playing a character can be effective. Think of someone whom you would like to emulate and imagine how that person would respond to certain situations—and then execute that behaviour accordingly. With time, you'll incorporate that behaviour into your usual repertoire, so you will eventually have no need of the role-play character because those target behaviours will have become yours. It can also be a useful way of developing or acquiring certain traits that you've consciously decide to focus on. It's not a matter of mirroring a single person's every move and gesture, but of selecting specific, tailored approaches to the way you respond to certain situations.

Make your own luck

Luck—by its very definition—is chancy, but you can improve the odds of having things fall in your favour. By having the right people around you and taking an optimistic mindset, you'll be able to make your own luck. However, remember that you need to 'be in it to win it'; in other words, if you want to obtain the outcomes of good luck, you have to raise your hand and become actively involved in making it happen.

When you're a positive, motivated person, you'll draw people—of all backgrounds—with similar dispositions to you. The people you attract may be the ones who provide you with the opportunity you've been looking for or the information vital to your journey. Or perhaps you will attract someone who will be a partner for the rest of your life. When you're feeling confident and positive, you develop a mindset that encourages you to obtain opportunities and information and then use them to your advantage. It also enables you to back yourself and your skills as you embark on new and deeply satisfying relationships.

By knowing where you're going and how you're getting there—and then launching yourself along that path—you'll exponentially increase your likelihood of attracting good luck, just like bees to honey.

When you make yourself an irresistible temptation of positive energy, not only will you attract opportunity, but you'll also repel negativity—because people who prefer to wallow in gloom are far less likely to be attracted to enthusiasm. So you'll find yourself attracting similar souls to you—and that can generate in you a pervasive 'anything is possible' mindset.

Swallow snails speedily

Take risks when you need to and trust your inner instinct. Most of all, though, you just have to get on with it.

Anthony Rushton

On the topic of behaviours, swallow snails speedily—once you've made the decision to make changes to your behaviour, ensure that you implement them as soon as possible.

For example, a significant reason for the success of Graham Dixon, popular CEO of Queensland Cricket, is his ability to think efficiently, act quickly and keep moving—an approach to people and time management that is very effective. When an issue arises, he acknowledges and assesses the problem, formulates a response to it, and then he executes that response and moves on. This applied both to the everyday and the infrequent. Graham wastes no time in procrastination; he also comfortably seeks the counsel of others and confidently executes his decisions. He doesn't panic or overreact—even in the face of challenging situations.

Indeed, by overcoming the temptation of procrastination, Graham has gained the respect of staff and stakeholders alike. By practising this approach frequently, it is no longer effort intensive and has become second nature to him—as he says, 'That's just how I do things!'

There's only so much research and thinking you can do before it becomes counterproductive; in other words, within a reasonable period of time, you have to execute your decisions. Procrastination over difficult situations affects your levels of momentum—as well as people's views on your ability and dedication. Not only are you prevented from carrying out your plans by procrastination, but, additionally, others around you will start to question your abilities or your dedication to the outcome.

On avoiding procrastination, when I enquired of Butter Bistro's personable owner, Anthony Rushton, how he would advise others on success, he illustratedpromptly declared, 'Oh, just get on with it! You have to be yourself and do what you think is right.

Acting quickly, on the other hand, does not mean acting impulsively and without thought; an appropriate time limit should be applied to assessing the situation at hand and formulating an approach. Set yourself the time to do that. Once that approach has been formulated, again set yourself a time limit within which to implement it. You will then maintain the wave of momentum required to achieve your goal, before moving forward and on to your next challenge.

Whether you want to make changes to your routine or control the less attractive but essential tasks, it's best to do it quickly. (Tony Wilson has a valuable piece of advice on this point; he says that it's important to 'set up daily processes and do the things that you least like first of all'.) Below are some strategies for incorporating these changes into your life:

- If you need to allocate time to new activities, write up a weekly schedule and put it somewhere highly visible. Allocate specific times in your diary for any activities that are in addition to those that you usually undertake—and make those time slots non-negotiable until they become habitual. Try to write up your weekly schedule at the same time each week.

- Regular activities—such as switching on your computer or cleaning your teeth—can be effective reminders. Attach any new activities to activities that you usually undertake—such as an early-morning walk. By attaching new activities to your regular ones, you'll develop and consolidate the new activities into one routine.

- A diary or journal can also be very helpful to track your successes or hiccups while making changes along the way. By recording your thoughts on your progress—even just by giving yourself a 'satisfaction rating' about how you feel you've progressed—you'll be able to view your progress. It will also enable you to identify regular pitfalls and work out why some things aren't working out as you had planned.

- Make sure you reward yourself for any efforts you make in a positive direction. Minimise the time you spend criticising yourself for not meeting your targets straightaway.

Ponder points

- Sometimes following your path to achieve your goals requires sacrifice or forgoing the activities that others are free to do.

Ponder points (cont'd)

- Work smart—understand the most effective approach to execution and reward yourself when you achieve.

- Focus on process goals rather than outcome goals. Process goals should be within your full control; outcome goals are generally open to influence.

- Examine your habits. Which are contributing to goal success? Which are not and should be discarded?

- Be persistent. You're not always going to get to where you want to be in the time it takes for you to say, 'I'm a success!' Understand that it's often a long process that usually involves challenge along the way. Commit fully at the start in order to stay connected to the path throughout.

- Discipline your brain to avoid disaster thinking.

- Develop a clear picture of success in your mind and use it when your brain tends towards negativity.

- Develop an effective recovery routine. Match strategies to situations and to different points during the day.

- Do positive things to home in on your goal. Even when you don't feel altogether like doing them, ensure you do at least one positive activity.

- Develop a champion mindset—remain calm, analyse the situation, formulate a plan and execute that plan with conviction.

➤ Understand that planning and practice are vital to success. Properly factor in the time that it takes to do both.

➤ Serenade serendipity—maximise your luck by being 'attractive' to opportunity.

➤ Acquire the practice of maintaining your equilibrium regardless of outcome. In other words, choose not to over-celebrate your wins or over indulge the sadness of your losses.

➤ Have some strategies up your sleeve for overcoming adversity. Learn to anticipate pits of doom; use goal setting to reset yourself; ask for help when you need it; regularly review your progress; identify the anchors in your life; identify what it is that helps you to keep perspective.

➤ When you've decided to make changes, do so efficiently and effectively—and without procrastination.

Part III

Go

Chapter 7

Combine and conquer

You've now looked at each of the FFSS mindset elements —internal drivers, external drivers and behaviours—that contribute to your performance. This chapter provides you with some ways that others have used those elements to overcome challenges and adversity.

By harnessing all the elements you will be stronger because each element influences the others. Stories taken from sports, business and life show how you can combine and conquer challenges both small and large.

Keeping composure

If you can meet with Triumph and Disaster, and treat those two imposters just the same.

Rudyard Kipling

Keeping composure is vital when you need to deal with reasonable punishment. Elton Flatley, gives me a personal example:

> When I was dropped from the team [Wallabies] for playing up, it was a real kick in the pants. I remember seeing the test match at home alone with the kids. It was even worse when we lost—I felt I'd let the boys down.

Elton learned from that experience and it has made him significantly more professional in how he applies himself to training and playing. He's not about to make the mistake twice. He also had the fortitude to take the lesson on the chin, without feeling sorry for himself. A lot of rugby players over the years have been rapped over the knuckles for substandard behaviour and then promptly 'lost it'—dropped their discipline and dropped out of the game, despite huge talent. The chances are it was their one big opportunity to achieve in a sport they loved, but they choked at the first hurdle.

If you can meet 'Triumph and Disaster' with feedback, whether positive or negative, so long as it is constructive, longevity on your success path will be significantly enhanced. Recognise when a rap over the knuckles or constructive criticism is warranted and swallow the feelings that threaten to curtail your success. Take a deep breath, count to ten and go distract yourself by doing something constructive.

Maintaining your equilibrium is essential. An important part of that is validating feelings. I advise coaches that if the athlete or team has done poorly, they should acknowledge the pain of disappointment. Coaches should empathise and refrain from trying to mitigate the pain immediately. The same applies to the joy of a win. Players and their coaches should acknowledge the delight of winning—which is much easier to do than feeling comfortable with sorrow—and allow those moments. Then, when arousal levels have settled—regardless of a win or a loss—coaches and their team should engage in a debrief—covering questions such as what went well? What didn't go well? How do we improve for next time? This debriefing allows a critical return to a balanced view of the event.

Practise the same for yourself at the end of each day or after an event worth pondering. Acknowledge your feelings because it's from these that people learn. Then take the same approach to critiquing your performance—regardless of whether you had a 'win' or a 'loss'. Finally, change your focus in anticipation of the next event.

Overcoming adversity

The real victory was wrested less from flesh and blood than from the pitiless ordeal of shellfire and from that inexorable opponent, General Mud, in his home country, Flanders. But, do its worst, it failed to quench the spirit.

Donald Banks

My grandfather, Donald Banks, was an exceptionally talented man in a number of areas. His quote, taken from his memoirs and notes on his first-hand military experiences, demonstrates his acuity about the 'real opposition' of World War I—the mud of Flanders in which so many lives were lost to illness and infection. Happily, times have changed, but the lesson remains—when in battle, in any battle, it's vital to be aware of your foremost opposition (and that opponent may not necessarily be the most obvious nor the only one). This is when your research into your path ahead can really reap dividends, or, at the very least, minimise trouble. Aside from anything else, if you know what you're up against, you stand a greater chance of tackling it without the disadvantage of surprise.

'Never have a hungi without a fire extinguisher', offers restaurateur Anthony Rushton when asked his advice on preparation. He makes the remark about New Zealand's traditional inground barbeque only half in jest. Knowing your likely pits of doom in connection to any undertaking and preparing for them can help to avert disaster. If you're an expert in something you're about to undertake, you're less likely to need all the pieces of equipment recommended in the manual—because you've done the job plenty of times before and you are fully aware of what you need. (When planning a holiday, for example, you often know what you need to bring—right down to a bottle opener!) However, if it's a first-time experience, equip yourself well for the challenge. Hopefully, you may never need your accumulated preparations. Nevertheless, it's preferable to never need to open your first-aid kit than it is to need it but lack its presence.

The same principle can be applied to other areas of your life—it's better to over-prepare for the unfamiliar than risk under performance through being caught out. For example, if you're due to have a meeting and you think you're likely to feel overwhelmed or inarticulate, plan what you're going to say. Be clear on your intended goal for the meeting; write down key dot points and explain each point clearly and succinctly in your notes. Take your dot points into the meeting as a reference tool Maybe you won't need them, but at least they'll be available if you do.

For many of those raw recruits in World War I, heading into the marshes of Flanders was something they could never prepare for, and yet—as Grandpa pointed out—their spirit battled on. You can hypothesise and say that perhaps it was because they had a purpose; they knew what it was they were there for and they had a clear role to fulfil. Yet for many, that purpose became blurred with the passing of time. Rather, it was the camaraderie—their support teams—within a unit that lived, slept, fought and died together that carried them through that living nightmare. Even in the depths of darkness, human beings have the capacity to gain strength from each other—even by finding humour in the bleakest of situations. An excerpt from the *Australian War Diaries* bears testament to some of the humour that carried the Diggers through World War II:

> Miraculously there were no casualties, though bullets tore through clothing and equipment on many occasions. If it had

been less serious, that [river] crossing would have been amusing. We laughed about it later and we laugh about it now.

When you're looking straight down the barrel, facing a nightmare of your own, then the best key to your survival is the presence of your support team. If you're anticipating significant trouble, then place priority on assembling those vital energy sources around you sooner rather than later. At least then you'll be facing adversity with preselected quality and numbers on your side.

After the blast

For most people who have faced adversity, the initial task after trouble hit was to fight the battle of the mind to take responsibility for their own successes and failures. This is illustrated by Janine Shepherd who says:

> Life doesn't owe us anything. No-one was actually going to lift my legs and build my muscles. It was up to me. The buck stopped with me. You have to take responsibility for your own personal growth. I died and came back in that accident and that experience was a great resource. It brought home to me that we're in control of our own destiny.

These were extraordinary words from a woman who has not only been challenged physically and emotionally by a life-changing accident, but who has also battled the rollercoaster of having a partner diagnosed with bipolar disorder and then the turmoil of separation from him. When asked about her method for coping, she replies, 'Every problem has a life span. Nothing is forever, including the bad stuff'.

Back to goal setting

So you accept that problems are finite, but where to from there? Janine has a few more comments to make on crisis recovery:

> I'm lucky that I have a goal-oriented personality. I've always set goals as an athlete and they're the things that have got me

through the hurdles and mountains that I've had through life. Once I was out of hospital, I set myself the goal of learning to fly. First, I set myself the target of getting my private pilot's licence. Once I had that, I concentrated on my instructor's licence. It's my goals that get me out of bed every morning.

Having worked with so many people both during and after they've experienced significant challenges in their life, I firmly believe that setting targets is one of the most crucial initial steps in overcoming the seemingly impossible.

Priorities

George Gregan, gives an example of prioritisation in goal resetting when working under pressure:

> In the Australia versus England game in 2004, England was in the lead with fifteen minutes to go. We were under pressure, but the boys locked in on what they could control and each individual took responsibility for their bit.

As with any team operation, there are a considerable number of possible directions to go in. For success, it's essential to rapidly sort through and prioritise those options—allocating greater importance to directions that can be controlled. The intense pressure of a test match provides a relevant example of the importance of focusing on your priorities and on changing the things that are within your control.

Eddie Jones is frank when talking about the professional challenge of being removed from his Australian coaching job with the Wallabies:

> The first thing I learned was that when you're sacked, people start to look at you as though you've committed murder, as though you've done something dreadfully wrong. Once I'd got past that initial stage, I focused on what I really wanted to do which was to give something back to Australian rugby. I've had offers from overseas for a lot more money, and perhaps one day I'll accept one of those offers, but until then, I want to see

Queensland go well. I want to make it strong. It'll be good for Australian rugby and will give added meaning to what I do.

When faced with a significant professional challenge, Eddie turned his mind back to his goals and what he wanted to really achieve. Once he'd clarified that, he was able to reset his career path and choose the option that best fitted that target.

Career turns are a challenge, but there's nothing quite like crisis and disaster to hone your focus on priorities. My mother, Irene Darling, lost her husband—and my siblings and I lost our father—in an accident when we, her children, were aged nine, seven and four years old. It was devastatingly unexpected. We were unprepared emotionally and financially. For the first time, this year, I talked to her about the impact that trauma had on her personally. She said:

> It was a huge shock. None of us—least of all your father—had contemplated such a tragedy happening to the family. We'd always shared the role of raising the family, but now I had the harsh reality of doing it on my own. It was heartbreaking from every angle. Piggy, your father, just never thought he'd die, or at least not for a long time. There were no funds in the bank for the future and no provisions made. He lived life so confidently—I suppose we all did.

> I knew that I had to get on with it though, so I asked myself, 'What's important in life? What's going to get me through?' As a mother, I'm responsible for these three children. I have to keep life running along; I have to be a rock to the children, no matter how it feels inside. So I focused on being a foundation of stability—children are dependent on a leader and I was the only one left to lead.

Having identified her key priority of bringing up her children, she then turned to the 'how' of doing it—as demonstrated by her comments below:

> I had to keep the business running in order to bring up my children in the way I wanted. This wasn't easy since I had

the added burden of convincing others of the viability of the business since I was a woman in a man's world. The bank froze the accounts. People would ring up and ask to speak to the director. When I said, 'Speaking', they'd hang up. It was really hard. But I felt that what I was doing was right, not wrong—and it was for the sake of the children and for the sake of Piggy's memory. I remembered the tough early days of starting the business together and I didn't want it to be thrown away. I suppose thanks to those early days, I remembered how to overcome dramas—little successes increased my confidence in myself and my ability.

To hear my mother talk about being low on confidence gave me a start; this was a woman who'd been one of the first female steeplechase jockeys in England—she wouldn't bat an eyelid at soaring over huge fences almost twice her height at warp speed on a horse only slightly under control. But this time around, it was about consequences that mattered more to her; if the business didn't work, it was her children's future that was at stake and that mattered more to her than anything she'd encountered previously. An extraordinary woman, she said that, after twelve months, she 'realised that the business would succeed and the children's futures were safe'. She has indeed been a tremendously stable foundation and leader for her family.

My mother isn't the only person who's told of their tale of trauma suffered and ultimately conquered. From Janine Shepherd and AnneMarie White's personal tales of courage, to the battles encountered by clients and friends, the stories in this book should give insight into how to strategise your encounters with challenges.

Crisis and pressure undeniably focus the mind on the vital priorities. You only have a limited amount of energy—especially during challenging times—and prioritisation allows you to funnel that energy in the direction it is most required.

Asking for help

Once you've nailed your priorities and worked out what needs to be done, you need to check whether you require assistance from others. Many people dislike asking for aid because they feel it reflects poorly on their capacity to cope with a situation. However, the more discerning in the population recognise when the provision of external assistance is vital to produce a successful outcome.

Paul McLean, ARU President, discloses his personal experiences of asking for help:

> I had depression about nine years ago and lost a stone in weight. I talked it through with my GP, who also happened to be my neighbour. We discussed everything openly and within six to eight months, I'd overcome the depression, had increased stability in my work and increased confidence in myself. I'm not saying that it was easy to do, but the point is, you need to recognise when you have to ask for help and then actually go and do it.

The point about asking for help—and about asking it from the right sources—is that it acts as a catalyst for change. It is about recognising the need for additional knowledge and application of that knowledge and how that process speeds up recovery and achievement.

There is still a certain mindset in the community that I find baffling—when someone breaks a leg, no-one would hesitate to seek assistance from a doctor to have it treated, yet when the mind is wounded but there appears to be nothing physically amiss, people can be loath to seek help. Human beings have struggled for centuries to understand and accept the things they cannot see—after all, it required the invention of a microscope before the concept of a germ was even accepted by the greater scientific community.

But simply because some of your struggles and challenges are internal and mental—and therefore intangible—does not mean they cannot lead to the disease of disaster. It is far better to ask for treatment than run the risk of deteriorating into something far worse. In the same vein, the declaration, 'Oh, it's only in your head' implies that mental health is less important than physical health. But what an understatement! If something is 'in someone's head', then it can be as stubborn to remove as the toughest nut grass and equally as infectious. Remember that a problem acknowledged is a problem half-conquered; a problem denied is a problem alive and kicking and having babies.

I'm referring to professional assistance here, but not necessarily to that of the medical variety. When there are challenges at work, it can be effective to garner managerial aid; when there are money issues, it's useful to ask for financial advice. Naturally, not all challenges require assistance from other people, but the key to success lies in recognising when they do—and acting on it.

Review and refocus

If you can make a heap of all your winnings and risk it on a turn of pitch and toss and lose, and start again at your beginnings, but never breathe a word about your loss.

Rudyard Kipling

The importance of a review procedure and the value of taking the same debriefing approach regardless of outcome is discussed early in the book; here ARU referee Scott Young talks about how this relates to his line of work:

> You need to be realistic…when you make a large number of decisions; the chances are that some of them at some point won't be the best ones. You need to accept human fallibility—to shut the door and move on. I force myself to focus on process not the outcome—like not looking up at the screen for replays,

but refocus to the next set of play. If you allow a mistake to distract you, it's basically like making a mistake twice.

Reviewing is exactly what's required to help put you back on track. Ask yourself what was done poorly—it's easy to nail in disaster situations—but also look at what was done well. It can be hard to ascertain in a crisis, but being aware of your strengths is vital for continuing along the road to success. You need to be clear on your strengths in order to use them effectively. An excellent example of how important it is to acknowledge your successes is set in the Queensland dressing-rooms after the first Super 14 rugby game in 2006. The New South Wales side had just won a game that was tight, brutal and intense. The Queensland Reds players were understandably gutted because they'd played with heart and soul. John Roe, the Reds' captain, drew the players into a circle and called over all the support staff. He and Chris Latham then delivered one of the most inspiring post-competition talks that I've ever heard. They acknowledged the pain of loss, but they applauded the effort, intensity and amazing sense of team. Latham declared, 'Hold your heads up! You should be proud. We played as a team and we took it to them'. Roe and Latham pointed out the team cohesion displayed by the players. As a result, the boys continued to move forward while using skills such as talking positively and supporting one another, and deriving energy from recognising that despite losing, they still have strengths to build on.

Given that the previous Reds season had been uninspiring in its results and that the team had been criticised for a lack of cohesion, the boys that night were all worthy of winning a game that many people had presumed would result in the New South Wales side delivering carnage. However, despite a tight scoreline, a win to Queensland was not to be. Latham and Roe—echoing sentiments made earlier by coach Jeff Miller—were exceptional in their management of a heart-breaking situation. Rather than allowing themselves to focus on the final score, they forced each player to acknowledge his significant and positive contribution and challenged each person to remember the standard set that night and to carry it through into the games ahead. It was a privilege for me to bear witness to that display and see such a change in team atmosphere from the previous year.

Of course, acknowledging strengths in the face of poor results is one thing, but what if the bad things flatly refuse to behave quietly in your head? Well, first, you need to ask whether you have derived all the lessons learned from your 'unsuccesses'. Have you identified what needs to be done to rectify things in the future—and have you made that a part of your ongoing strategy?

Second, you need to engage in some thought stopping. Perpetually recalling your deficiencies is a form of mental self-flagellation. You may do it to appease guilt—you stuffed up, so you think that by continuing to bash yourself, you may eventually feel better. It's a very medieval and ineffective approach. Alternatively, you may have the mental discipline of a caterpillar in a cabbage patch and simply allow yourself to wallow in thoughts wherever they may lead—rather than taking a more proactive approach and asserting your authority over them.

Mental undiscipline is prevalent—being characterised by the attitude of someone who thinks, 'I think; therefore, I think whatever I want and whenever I want'. Regular meditation practice can set some firm foundations for disciplined thought because you'll get faster and more effective at sending your thoughts in a particular direction and holding them there. Alternatively, increasing your self-awareness is an invaluable skill. Simply by regularly being aware of what's going through your mind, you can practise stopping your thoughts and sending them in an entirely different, but predetermined, direction.

Naturally, one of the keys is to know the mental direction you're going to focus on. Frankly, it doesn't really matter what you choose—as long as it's positive in some regard and decided upon ahead of time. If you haven't, then you're likely to fail in maintaining your thought-stopping efforts. You can pull out the weeds, but if you don't have a strong seed plant handy, those weeds will quickly return.

Going back to the issue of negative things revolving around in your head, to effectively whack a wedge in the 'hamster wheel' of your thoughts, identify your alternative 'thought focus'. You can post reminders to yourself about it or establish visual cues to remind you of it — try yelling, 'Stop!' inside your head; and then assertively send your brain in the direction that you've chosen. If there's any sign of your thoughts descending into doom again, repeat the procedure. Eventually, you'll become very effective at it.

Anchors during storms

Grief is the agony of an instant; the indulgence of grief the blunder of a life.

Benjamin Disraeli

Overcoming adversity requires a multipronged approach. Managing challenges effectively is important, but of equal importance is being able to survive and maintain your energy levels. That's where anchors come into play. Just as an anchor in a storm allows a ship to steady herself and maintain position, so too do the anchors in your life keep you on stable footing.

Anchors are essentially the stable elements in your life. Reviewing your life wheel can help you to identify those stable spots. It's very rare to live a life that is completely unstable in all areas. For example, you may be having trouble at work, but your family life could be strong. Alternatively, you may be having trouble at home and work, but have a great leisure pastime. Use those stable spots to anchor your emotions and feelings. Spend time in those areas in order to boost your energy and allow some recovery in order to face the storms of adversity. Spend time reflecting on the strengths and smiles associated with those anchors as well. People have a propensity to think, 'That stuff's going right, so I need to concentrate my attention on the stuff that isn't'. It's true that people need to focus their attention on areas for development, but they garner the energy to do that from the anchors in their lives.

Still on challenges, Ben Darwin had an accident on the rugby field that seriously injured his neck. At the time, he could feel nothing from his neck down and, while lying on the ground, he thought to himself, 'I'm going to die'. Here Ben describes how he tackled the challenge of that potentially life-threatening injury:

> After that moment, I had some huge changes in my thinking and realised what was really important in my life. My career as a professional rugby player was finished, but that wasn't important, all of a sudden. I lost my self-consciousness and I now find joy in life more easily. I enjoy the simple pleasures of life—love from family and friends, and time with my dog—simplicity.

Although Ben readily admits he still has a way to go to work out where the next part of his life is going to take him, he's confident that if he does what he loves doing—coaching others both on and off the rugby field—then the good things will come. The fact that his dream of one day being the world's greatest tighthead prop is unfulfilled is something he won't make, in Disraeli's words, 'the blunder of a life'. In light of Ben's remarks, AnneMarie White's memories of the day she was diagnosed with cancer resonate clearly:

> On the Friday I was told that I had breast cancer. My family were all up and, for the duration of the weekend, I allowed myself to indulge in all the negative thoughts—up until my daughter flew back home on the Monday afternoon. I then made myself sit down and make a list of all the things I'd need to do for all possible scenarios. If I die, what would I need to have in place? If I live and have to go through surgery, what would I need to do? I wrote down a really detailed plan.
>
> I'm not saying that it was all plain sailing. With cancer, there are terror moments, but when those happened, I'd make myself do something. That way, I was taking control of myself and my life.

It also meant that I had the courage to keep moving forward as I had already 'dealt with' the thoughts of worst case scenario.

The final piece of advice on avoiding 'poor me syndrome' should be left to my friend Phil Hogan, who says:

> Life isn't fair. Look! You have a kid who's now an orphan because he's lost his family and home to a tsunami. And then there's Paris Hilton. Of course life isn't fair, so don't expect it to be. Life doesn't owe you anything — the negatives are all a part of the game, so take the hand that you're dealt and deal with it. It's all up to you.

It's about perspective

Challenges and crises in the early stages may well facilitate your successes in the long term. Ben Tune has some relevant remarks on the topic:

> I matured late. I was small throughout high school and immediately afterwards. Being underdeveloped as a footballer and probably with a bit of a case of small man's syndrome, I wanted to prove that just because I was small, I could still achieve. My parents said to me that I'd actually play my better games against bigger opposition. They were right. It's all about how you look at things and the attitude that you take into the game. I've had three major knee operations and six minor ones. Yes, it's pretty bad, but there are more important things in life. To complain about a few knee operations, well, I think that's a bit rich. At the very least, hide your emotions when you're in public! Keep a balanced view of your place in the world. Don't over-estimate what you're doing — and that's especially relevant to sportspeople. It's not like we're curing cancer.

John Roe, Ben's team captain and a final-year medical student, echoes Ben's words:

> Footy isn't a real job. I'm lucky to do what I love. It's so important to keep in mind that it's just a game, even though I want to

perform at my best. It's not like you're a surgeon where you can make a real impact on people's lives. I'm privileged to be doing what I do, but my wife is a doctor and that's serious. Being around people who do have a real impact on others' lives allows you to have perspective on your own situation.

As John has learned, by gaining perspective, it can relieve your mind of the pressure it may feel regarding the outcome of your performance. So if the outcome is deemed to be less vital, then the implied threat of failure is also significantly reduced.

There are times when you need to be able to shrug off the small stuff and remember that you're generally not curing cancer. Sometimes people become so caught up in the hurly-burly of everyday life that they work themselves into a sweat over the small stuff—even though those matters are only little and relatively unimportant. Life usually succeeds in throwing people plenty of challenges that are indeed pivotal. So it's crucial that you save your energy reserves for the times when you can really make a difference to outcomes that could be life-changing.

◻   ◻   ◻

You can only control what you have the capacity to control. You have limited energy and resources, so you need to assign them wisely. Your first step when facing a challenge—apart from assembling your support team—is to find out exactly what you're looking at. Make some effort on your exploration platform—even if time is short—to work out whether the 'beast', or challenge, has four or eight heads, a single eye or an Achilles heel. Learn more about how to tackle it from multiple information sources and then develop an effective plan that will maximise the longevity of your energy, so that you can fight the challenge as long as it's required. Remember also that the best intentions in the world will come to nothing if you don't conduct sufficient recovery and therefore can't face the following day.

When tackling breast cancer, AnneMarie White took the time to learn all about the challenge ahead of her. She spent time with oncologists and researched the disease and how best to face it. She gathered her friends about her, who were nicknamed the FOAMs (friends of AnneMarie), and gained support from them. She learned that the treatment process was going to be exhausting both mentally and physically, so she planned ahead for when she was going in for a visit—ensuring that she had something to do to help her recovery afterwards. She formulated her plan and she stuck to it with the help of her family and friends—and she came out the other side of illness with a clear bill of health. Of course, there were dark moments during her journey—she is quick to admit to them—but she had the mental recovery strategies in place and the determination to ride them out.

The key lessons, aside from having a terrific support team, are clear—know what you're up against, develop a plan of attack while being clear on your BOMOAG and stick to your pathway with the help of some strategies. *Fitter, Faster, Stronger, Smarter* is about regaining your sense of control and ability to *do* something—rather than simply being the passive recipient of whatever fate happens to dish out.

Ponder points

➽ Do you maintain your composure in the face of triumph or disaster? Do you approach your challenges with equilibrium?

➽ The first hurdle when facing challenge is usually the tidal wave of gloom and negativity that sucks away hope and strength. Develop your awareness of that feeling and openly challenge it in your mind.

Ponder points (*cont'd*)

» Know your opposition and prepare for the battle ahead.

» Accept that all problems have a lifespan—and, like the good times, the bad times will pass.

» Reset your goals when things go awry and ask for help when you need it.

» Learn to take a macro view of your life and identify the anchors that give you strength and stability—even when other areas in your life are tumultuous.

» Develop perspective. How important is your challenge in the overall scheme of your life? If the answer is, 'Huge', face the challenge systematically, step by step, and try to take back the control that it wrested from you.

The final note

So you've managed to work your way through to these last few pages. You've had opportunities to ponder and chances to write up your to do lists. You now have the tools for constructing your success map.

I discussed earlier the importance of setting goals that were your own, implementing review times for your progress along your success map and of believing in your ability and method in achieving your goals. Staying on track with the FFSS mindset also requires similar principles—are you acquiring the FFSS mindset for your own powerful reasons? Have you set review times? Do you believe in your ability to acquire and maintain the FFSS mindset to help you achieve your goals?

The next step is to check that you have a realistic perspective of your journey and have made plans to manage the slow patches or times when you've fallen off the path. Ensure that you have briefed your support team on your intentions and feel comfortable with asking for your team's assistance. Surround yourself with reminders of your direction and your end goal.

From here, it's up to you. After all, each person I spoke to about achievement said that it is necessary to take responsibility for your own success. So although there may be supportive people around you, responsibility for the outcomes of your performance rests on your shoulders alone.

I suggest that you review the ponder points at the end of each chapter. Use the example success map as a guide to formulate your own one if you need to. Set your review times, modify your environments and make notes in your diary—do whatever it is you have to do to align yourself and your behaviours with your BOMOAG.

This book is designed to be a reference tool as well as a method to provoke your thinking, so put it somewhere convenient and make it as dog-eared as you need it to be. Perhaps think of it as a travel guide to your journey of performance through life. Feel free to add in your own learning and modify my suggestions to fit your own situation, just as you'd do with any guidebook. Life is dynamic and the tools you use to engender your best performances should reflect the same dynamism.

When I give talks around the country, my echoing challenge to the audience members is the same that I pose to you now—from this moment forward, start by making at least one change to how you do things. Everyone can improve. Even the best athletes in the world have a coach—because they know that there will always be room for improvement.

You too can have your support team—perhaps even your own coach to assist you along your pathway—but there's only one body who's with you 100 per cent of the time—you. You're your own engine and driver, so you'll see no action if you don't act—and making changes is the hardest of all when it's only you around.

I'll leave you to embark on your pathway, with a final inspirational story that illustrates the power of the FFSS approach. I was at an induction camp for all newly contracted professional rugby players. We'd gathered in Sydney from the other rugby states. The boys spent much of their time in workshops both on and off the field—being addressed by experts who were integral to professional rugby.

Now, young rugby players, like most young lads and lasses, are not renowned for their powers of concentration in classroom environments. They tend to 'switch on' for their topics of preference, but otherwise spend much of their time floating in the clouds somewhere out the second window on the right. There was one particular moment at that camp, however, that remains in my memory because it truly captivated their attention.

Jason Weber, the longstanding strength and conditioning trainer for the Wallabies, had come in to have a quick word to the boys about expectations. Now Jason is a strapping chap with a happy disposition, though he doesn't suffer fools. He stood up in front of the room and was clear and succinct about the things he was looking for in future international players.

He talked about how vital it is to be self-motivated about making change and not relying upon others to propel you into action. He also talked about the importance of working hard, even when there is no coach or trainer around to monitor performance.

With a question to the players in his closing comments, he succeeded in gaining the boys' full and wrapt attention—all eyes were on him. It was a simply question that I will also pose to you:

What are *you* doing to achieve your goals when nobody else is watching?

Appendix A
A success map framework

My purpose in life is:

_____

_____

_____

_____

My BOMOAG is:

_____

_____

_____

_____

This will be achieved by:

_____

_____

_____

_____

The values in which I believe are:

_____

_____

_____

_____

The milestone goals along my journey are, in chronological order:

1 _____

2 _____

3 _____

4 _____

5 _____

These will be achieved by:

_____

_____

_____

_____

My progress will be reviewed at the following times:

_____

_____

_____

_____

The skills and knowledge that I need to acquire are:

_____

_____

_____

_____

I shall acquire them by:

_____

_____

_____

_____

The behaviours that I need to achieve my goals are:

Positive-action behaviours:

_____

_____

_____

_____

Recovery behaviours:

_____

_____

_____

_____

The attitudes that I need to achieve my goals are:

_____

_____

_____

_____

My support team is:

_____

_____

_____

_____

The energy pumps in my life are:

_____

_____

_____

_____

The energy parasites in my life are:

_____

_____

_____

_____

If I was to choose a role model, that person would be:

_____

_____

_____

_____

If I was to choose a mentor, that person would be:

_____

_____

_____

_____

I shall maximise my geographical environments by:

_____

_____

_____

_____

I shall maximise my physical environments by:

_____

_____

_____

_____

I choose to start this success map on:

_____

_____

_____

_____

Appendix B

Phil Hogan's keys for success

- Keep your life balanced; family comes first.
- Stay focused; you must focus like a laser.
- Make sacrifices; everything has a price.
- Remember to have fun; it's only money.
- Shut up and listen; loose lips sink ships.
- Keep fit; healthy body, healthy mind.
- Eat healthy food; you are what you eat.
- Speak well; you must be positive and polite.
- Keep an open mind; always remain flexible.
- Try to co-operate; be proactive not reactive.
- Live within your means; waste not, want not.
- Be well presented; clean shoes and a tidy car.

- Visualise success; think, believe and become.
- Keep good company; avoid negative people.
- Pay attention to detail; strive for excellence.
- Work hard; people create their own luck.
- Employ great people; people are the key.
- Don't waste time; early to bed, early to rise.
- Set goals; write them down, review regularly.
- Be persistent; never quit, just keep going.
- Believe in yourself; your God is guiding you.
- Be an individual; don't just follow the herd.
- Take action; don't procrastinate, be decisive.
- Fear not; there are no failures, just outcomes.
- Accept responsibility; don't blame others.
- Give something back; it's far more rewarding.
- Dream big dreams; must be vivid and specific.
- Always believe that nothing is impossible!

Appendix C

A progressive muscular relaxation technique

The following steps provide you with a guide to one of my favourite effective progressive muscular relaxation (PMR) technique.

1   Ready yourself for bed and hop in. Ensure that the curtains are drawn and there are no distractions.

2   Focus on your breathing. Take two deep, calming breaths.

3   Now focus on your head—in particular, your face. Scrunch up your face muscles tightly. Hold them. Then relax them slowly, exhaling as you do so. Feel the tension flow out down through your body.

4   Next, focus on your neck and shoulders. Pull your shoulders up towards your ears as hard as you can. Hold them—and slowly release, exhaling at the same time. Feel the tension flow out down through your arms and out of your fingertips. Repeat if necessary.

5   Then focus on the top of your left arm—on your biceps and triceps. Scrunch them as hard as you can. Hold. Then relax slowly—feeling the tension flow out down through your left arm and out of your fingertips.

6   Now move down to your left forearm and hand. Make a fist with your hand and tighten it as hard as you can, while tightening the muscles in your forearm. Hold tight. Relax slowly—uncurl your fingers and feel the tension flow out through the tips of your fingers.

7   Repeat this procedure for your right arm.

8   Next, focus on your chest. Imagine that you have a tight band around your chest and that you're trying as hard as you can to use your chest muscles to force it off. Hold. Relax—feeling the tension flow away and out down through your body.

9   Now for your stomach. Pull in your stomach muscles as hard as you can. Hold. Relax.

10 Next, focus on the muscles in your bottom. Tense. Hold for a couple of seconds. Then relax—breathing out as you do.

11 Move down to your left leg. Focus on tensing your thigh muscles. Hold. Then relax as your exhale. Repeat with the calf muscles in your left leg—feeling the tension flow down your leg and out through your toes. Finally, scrunch up your toes. Hold. Then relax.

12 Repeat this procedure for your right leg—finishing up again by scrunching your toes and then slowly uncurling them.

13 Your body is now feeling completely relaxed and heavy. As you're lying there, imagine a comfortable warmth starting in your toes and slowly spreading its way up through your legs and body. It makes you feel very sleepy. Your breathing is rhythmic—being characterised by deep, slow breaths.

Index

If you found this book useful ...

... then you might like to know about other similar books published by John Wiley & Sons. For more information visit our website <www.johnwiley.com.au/trade>, or if you would like to be sent more details about other books in related areas please photocopy and return the completed coupon below to:

P/T Info
John Wiley & Sons Australia, Ltd
Level 3, 2 Railway Parade
Camberwell Vic 3124

If you prefer you can reply via email to:
<aus_pt_info@johnwiley.com.au>.

Please send me information about books on the following areas of interest:

- ❒ sharemarket (Australian)
- ❒ sharemarket (global)
- ❒ property/real estate
- ❒ taxation and superannuation
- ❒ general business.

Name:
Address:
Email:

Please note that your details will not be added to any mailing list without your consent.